George Martineau

Free Trade in Sugar

A Reply to Sir Thomas Farrer

George Martineau

Free Trade in Sugar
A Reply to Sir Thomas Farrer

ISBN/EAN: 9783744734264

Printed in Europe, USA, Canada, Australia, Japan

Cover: Foto ©ninafisch / pixelio.de

More available books at **www.hansebooks.com**

FREE TRADE

IN

SUGAR.

A Reply to Sir Thomas Farrer.

BY

GEORGE MARTINEAU.

" We do not seek free trade in corn primarily for the purpose of purchasing it at a cheaper money rate ; we require it at the natural price of the world's market, whether it becomes dearer with a free trade or whether it is cheaper, it matters not to us, provided the people of this country have it at its natural price, and every source of supply is freely opened, as Nature and Nature's God intended it to be ; then, and then only, shall we be satisfied."—*Speeches of Richard Cobden*, p. 105.

PUBLISHED FOR THE AUTHOR

BY

CASSELL & COMPANY, LIMITED:

LONDON, PARIS, NEW YORK & MELBOURNE.

1889.

CONTENTS.

APPENDIX A.

APPENDIX B.

APPENDIX C.

APPENDIX D.

APPENDIX E.

APPENDIX F.

PREFACE.

THOUGH it involves great repetition, I have, in the last four chapters of this pamphlet, replied, paragraph by paragraph, to the fresh matter in Sir Thomas Farrer's book. The earlier chapters are reprints of my published replies to those letters of Sir Thomas Farrer which were accepted by the *Times*.

I have thought it best to make myself solely responsible for the body of this little book. It is only for that reason that very interesting replies to Sir Thomas Farrer, from much abler pens than mine, are placed in the Appendix. I hope that they will not, on that account, escape the attention of the reader. Mr. Shepheard's treatment of the subject, from the Political Economist's point of view, is most valuable. The West Indians, and, in fact, all cane-sugar producers, are well represented in Mr. Lubbock's letters; and the Sugar House workmen must be proud of so able an advocate as Mr. Shute. Mr. Shepheard has also allowed me to reprint his legal examination of the bearing of most-favoured-nation treaties on the question.

GEORGE MARTINEAU.

April 3, 1889.

P.S.—Since writing the above, Lord Bramwell's letter has appeared in *The Times*. I have therefore added to the Appendix a short reply, which shows that his argument is entirely based on an erroneous assumption.

April 8, 1889.

INTRODUCTION.

AT the moment when this pamphlet is appearing, a "boom" is taking place in the sugar markets of the world. The leading market report in Mincing Lane says: "It is now evident, as was foreseen might be the case, that the holders on the Continent have the immediate future of the market much in their hands, owing to the reduction of stocks in Europe and America, as well as to the decrease in some of the leading sources of cane production." The bounty-fed source of supply is now master of the situation, and no wonder, seeing that its production is considerably more than double the total visible production of the world. This is the unnatural monopoly which, we are told, must not be interfered with, because such interference would make sugar dearer. Instead of which we find, not for the first nor the second time, that it is the beetroot monopoly which frequently causes an excessive rise in price; while at other times it brings about what Sir Thomas Farrer so truly describes as "glut, collapse, and ruin." Both these effects of artificial interference with trade and industry are, in Sir Thomas Farrer's opinion, so beneficial to the general community that, in the name of Cobden, they must be defended and maintained against the insidious attacks of those who only ask for free trade in sugar.

It seems from the tables furnished by the Board of Trade that when bounties first came upon the scene, about 1862, the annual beetroot sugar production amounted to 400,000 tons, and formed one-fifth of what the Board of Trade erroneously calls the total production. Ten years afterwards it amounted to 1,140,000 tons, which was more than one-third of the Board of Trade total. It is now 2,800,000 tons, which considerably exceeds half the true visible production of the world. In spite of these facts, Sir Thomas Farrer denies that beetroot has, to that extent, taken the place of cane-sugar in the world's consumption. The figures he appeals to to prove his case—which he calls Mr. Picton's return—are curiously chosen, and turn out to be unreliable. The Board of Trade witness before the Select Committee of 1880 brought forward similar figures, gathered from the same Board of Trade table. He was asked how it was that a figure given as representing the total West Indian production was actually less than the imports into the United Kingdom of West Indian sugar in the same year. He replied that he could not explain it, but would inquire into the matter. The result of his inquiry was the discovery that the table furnished by the Board of Trade only gave a portion of the West Indian production. This is the table from which Mr. Picton's recent return has been furnished. The error, which would have deceived the

Select Committee but for the vigilance of the Chairman, is now reproduced without hesitation.

The letters here reprinted from the *Times* are a complete answer to the position taken up by Sir Thomas Farrer, both on the question of the price of sugar and on the larger question of Free Trade. He has taken no notice of the main facts and arguments contained in my letters ; but he does not hesitate to reproduce the assertions which I have refuted, and even amplifies them to double their original length. When his book was announced, it was naturally supposed that he would direct his attention, in the first instance, to dealing with our published replies. Though there is plenty of fresh matter in his book, there is not a single allusion to my arguments. The fresh matter merely repeats, in various forms, the old assertions which I am fairly entitled to consider that I have refuted, until Sir Thomas Farrer shows that I have failed to do so. Hitherto he has not made even an attempt in that direction.

Cobden devoted all his energies to breaking down an artificial monopoly and establishing free trade in our markets. Sir Thomas Farrer devotes his to the defence of an equally artificial monopoly, and to the maintenance of protection to foreign producers on British markets. And yet he does not hesitate to put the name of Cobden on his title-page.

FREE TRADE IN SUGAR.

CHAPTER I.

REPLY TO SIR THOMAS FARRER'S FIRST LETTER.

SIR,—There is one statement in Sir Thomas Farrer's letter
which, as it is repeated four times, and is in fact the text
on which his whole remarks are based, requires to be
contradicted if your readers are not to be misled. The
effect of the Convention, he says, will be to make sugar
dearer here and cheaper in other countries. I have already
in my former letters pointed out that this is impossible.
This country receives sugar from all parts of the world, and
has 5,000,000 tons to choose from. Bounty-fed sugar is sold
at the same price as other sugar, and all other sugar is, and
must be, sold at the same price as bounty-fed sugar. The
only effect the Convention will have will be the general
abolition of bounties, which Sir Thomas Farrer declares to
be bad things. But though he makes this admission he
harps on the great benefit which our own people derive
from bounty-fed sugar. What is this benefit? Is it a good
thing artificially to stimulate production in one place, and
thereby hinder and discourage production all over the
world? Is it a good thing that consumers should be dependent on one particular crop to such an extent, that,
whenever it is slightly less prolific than usual, prices rise
50 per cent.? Until Sir Thomas Farrer answers these
questions he has no right to pretend that we are being

B

robbed of a benefit by the abolition of bounties ; and
unless he shows that there are two prices for sugar his
whole contention is baseless.

The other points in his letter are that the ascertaining
the existence and amount of a bounty is impossible ; that
the most-favoured-nation article in our treaties is an obstacle ; that retaliation is against our principles ; and that
the Convention restricts our freedom. I venture to point
out, as briefly as possible, that Sir Thomas Farrer is mis-
taken on all these points. There was a time when our
assertions as to the existence and amount of the bounties
were disputed—by Sir Thomas Farrer among others. But
now the foreign Governments have saved us further trouble
on this point by stating periodically the amount of their
bounties very accurately. So far from the most-favoured-
nation article being an obstacle, it turns out to be exactly
the reverse. It has been urged at the sittings of the Conference that a country having such a treaty with us can
properly complain that the admission of bounty-fed sugar
destroys the equality which the most-favoured-nation
article is intended to secure. As to retaliation, it is most
unfair to pretend that there is any parallel between the
absurd and useless policy of retaliating against protective
duties and the very simple and practical process of
destroying protection to foreign producers on British
markets by the method proposed in the Convention. The
one is easy and effectual, the other impossible and futile.
Moreover, there is no retaliation in securing a bounty for
the revenue, or in giving a security to the contracting
Powers that bounties shall no longer operate to their dis-
advantage. Lastly, how does the Convention restrict our
freedom ? Sir Thomas Farrer says it throws a doubt on
our advocacy of free imports. Why, then, do we prohibit
goods bearing false trade-marks? So long as bounties

continue it cannot be said that "free imports" apply to sugar. Those who import sugar must be prepared to compete with sugar which receives a subsidy. Is this freedom?

Having already addressed you on this subject, I should not have ventured again to trespass on your valuable space, but as Sir Thomas Farrer has taken for his axioms the very points which I had already disproved, and as the *ex cathedrâ* style of his letter is likely to carry great weight, I again beg for your kind indulgence.

CHAPTER II.

REPLY TO THE SECOND LETTER.

SIR,—Sir Thomas Farrer's second letter expands to three columns what he had previously said in one; but it does not, with one important exception to which I will presently refer, add a single new point or argument to those contained in his former letter, to which you kindly permitted me to reply. Sir Thomas Farrer has paid my arguments the greatest compliment he could by not noticing them.

His former letter was characterised by Mr. Gladstone as "weighty." The present one is full of brilliant and telling phrases, and Sir Thomas Farrer is no doubt right in thinking that they will answer his purpose better and be more likely to make progress with the public than the drier process of close reasoning or the accurate use of words.

Sir Thomas Farrer's contention, identical in both letters, may be divided into two main propositions, viz. :—

1. That the bounties are good things for this country, because they make sugar cheaper than it would otherwise be.

2. That the Convention for their abolition is a Protectionist measure, contrary to the principles of Free Trade.

These two points are amplified and reiterated in various forms and many taking phrases; but that is what they amount to. We have replied to them for years in letters to the Press, and counter-memorandums addressed to the Board of Trade, until we are quite ashamed to repeat the same language so frequently. No one has ever attempted to grapple with our arguments, and yet the same brilliant phrases continue to appear from time to time, and no doubt dazzle many a casual reader.

With regard to the first of these two short propositions to which Sir Thomas Farrer's four columns may be reduced, it is fortunate that he has now made an admission which goes far to cut the ground from under his own feet. "It is not the amount of the bounty," he points out, "but the relation which bounty-fed sugar bears to other sugar in quantity [and in price], which determines the effect of bounty-fed sugar upon the market." This, with the exception of the words which I have put in brackets, which appear erroneous, is exactly what I have always urged as the true state of the case, and I am glad that Sir Thomas Farrer has now adopted the same view, because it clears aways a host of misconceptions. It is not the amount of the bounty, but the increased production brought about by the bounty which affects the price of sugar. This being so, and I think no one can dispute the fact, much which follows might be omitted from Sir Thomas Farrer's letter. He quotes some passages from one of the many long memorandums of the Board of Trade, based on the assumption—now shown by his own reasoning to be erroneous—that the cheapness is to be measured by the amount of the bounty. The conclusions arrived at on that basis are, therefore, utterly erroneous and misleading, and it is curious that Sir Thomas Farrer should lay stress upon them immediately after showing by his own argument that they are based on false premises.

The facts with regard to the effect of bounties on prices are very distinct and simple. The bounties on production have unnaturally stimulated it; consequently the market has, from time to time, been temporarily glutted. This has been followed by the natural process of reduced production and a restoration of the equilibrium between

supply and demand. If bounties were to continue indefinitely, this would repeat itself until all natural
production disappeared and the world was supplied entirely
from bounty-fed sources. Practically, of course, this is impossible ; but theoretically it is the completion of the curve.
Now, in the swing of the pendulum between artificially
stimulated over-production and the reduction of stocks to
normal proportions, it is clear that the market will pass
for a short time through a period of low prices. If these
low prices were the result of natural instead of artificial
over-production, the remedy would take a natural course.
But with the disturbing element of bounties the course
taken by the industry is also abnormal, and, as I maintain, seriously hurtful to the interests of the consumer and
the nation at large. Instead of producers straining every
nerve to be foremost in the race, they are deterred by the
very natural feeling that, however highly they may farm,
however perfect their machinery may be, there is still the
bounty looming in the background, against which they
cannot contend by any amount of perfection in cultivation
or manufacture. What has the result been ? That, while
the production of beetroot has increased by leaps and
bounds, there has been very slight increase in the production of cane sugar. In other words, the whole of the
enormous yearly increase in the world's consumption has
been filled up by beetroot sugar, stimulated by bounties.
The injurious result to the consumer has been illustrated
several times during the last few years. A short beetroot
crop means now a rise of 50 per cent. in the price of
sugar.

So much for the bounties on production. The bounties
on refining affect prices in an entirely different way. The
refiner depends solely on the margin between the price of
raw and refined. It is to him immaterial, from that point

of view, what price he gives for his raw sugar. He knows that he and his competitors all get it at the same price, and that he must get such a price for his refined as will pay the cost of refining, and leave him on the right side. A penny per ton, or any other fraction you like to mention, will therefore turn the scale between profit and loss in his case, and this fraction, though ruin to him, is quite inappreciable to the consumer. In his case, moreover, this process of underselling by a mere fraction below cost price is continuous, instead of coming, as in the case of the producer, in short periods of low prices followed by a rebound of the pendulum.

So far as bounties on refining are concerned, therefore, the consumer (including the jam and confectionery maker) makes no appreciable gain from bounties, and will suffer no appreciable loss by their abolition.

The bounties on production, on the other hand, cause the market to be periodically glutted, during which period the consumer gets his sugar for a short time at a low price. But he has to pay so much the more when the pendulum swings in the opposite direction, since he becomes each time more and more dependent on the beetroot crop; the practical result of which has been that several times during the last few years he has had to pay an advance of 50 per cent. But a far more serious effect, as I have pointed out, has been that all natural enterprise among cane-sugar producers has been paralysed, natural progress in manufacture stifled, and natural extension of cultivation hindered and discouraged. Sir Thomas Farrer wishes that this artificial hindrance to progress should continue, and he advocates it not only in the interests of the consumer, but, more extraordinary still, in the name of Free Trade!

If you will allow me, I will give my reply to Sir Thomas Farrer's other point in a second letter.

SIR.—I hope I have succeeded, in my replies to Sir Thomas Farrer, in showing that bounties are not, as he contends, good for us, but that, on the contrary, they are bad for the consumer as well as for the producer. I will now deal with his other main point, and show that the Convention for the suppression of these bounties is not, as Sir Thomas Farrer desires his readers to believe, in any way contrary to the strictest principles of Free Trade, but that, on the contrary, it is the only means by which Free Trade in sugar can be restored. I admit that all this has been proved *ad libitum* in reply to the same assertions when emanating from the Board of Trade, and I fearlessly assert that no attempt has ever been made by that department to meet our arguments. But, unfortunately, the readers of Sir Thomas Farrer's brilliant letters in your columns are not aware of this, and I fear that, with many, smart sentences go further than dry argument. I hope, however, that any one who will give a moment's reasonable consideration to the subject, unbiased by the unaccountable influence of party spirit which seems to have distorted the vision even of some clear-sighted people with regard to this purely scientific question, will admit at the outset that the effect of foreign bounties on articles imported into this country is to protect the foreign producer on our markets —that is, to give him an artificial advantage here over other producers. This is clearly a flagrant outrage on Free Trade principles, and no amount of eloquence or strong language ought to blind the eyes of reasonable people to the fact, or make them fancy that the removal of this protection to foreigners on British markets is in any way inconsistent with Free Trade principles. On the contrary, it might naturally be supposed that every reasonable man would at once exclaim, " It is evidently absolutely necessary, if Free Trade in sugar is to be maintained in this country,

that these bounties should be abolished, neutralised, or prohibited." So long as they continue to operate on our
markets they have the same effect as if a differential duty
were levied on all sugar not bounty-fed. The word
" Protection," as used in connection with Free Trade,
means an artificial advantage given to one producer over
another, and we Free-traders maintain that it is wrong in
principle and injurious in practice that any such artificial
advantage should exist, even when it is conferred on our
own producers. How much more must it be wrong in
principle and injurious in practice when the artificial advantage is conferred on the foreigner to the detriment of
the British producer in his own market. But, though we
destroy Free Trade, we get our sugar so wonderfully cheap!
That is what Sir Thomas Farrer, the Board of Trade, and
the Cobden Club have always fallen back upon when
driven into this corner. This I have already disposed of
by showing that there is no appreciable gain even in the
supposed temporary cheapness ; and that any artificial
cheapness involves a diversion of the current of production,
which must end in the loss or great reduction of the
natural sources, and the consequent dependence of the
consumer on artificial sources of supply. The sugar
bounties have already lasted long enough to give practical
illustrations of this fact, several serious rises having
occurred in the market in recent years, owing to the constantly increasing dependence of consumers on the success
of the beetroot crop.

The reasonable reader, to whom I have already ap-
pealed, would conclude that Sir Thomas Farrer, after these
points had been made clear, would be disposed to modify
his views. And there can be no doubt that under ordinary
conditions of discussion, with the single view of arriving
at the truth, this would be so. · But, as it is, we have still

the same mirage of politics hovering over our unfortunate
sugar question. Hence such phrases in Sir Thomas Farrer's
last letter as the following :—" Our English Minister,
misled by his Protectionist leanings, puts down foreign
bounties, not because they plunder the German taxpayers,
but because they give cheap sugar to his own countrymen."
" Keen-sighted for the narrow interests of a small producing class ; blind to the wide interests of a great consuming and producing nation ; masquerading as a Free-
trader, but in fact a Protectionist ; " and so on. This is
not dealing with an abstract question of political economy
in a scientific way, but simply following out the old rule of
abusing the attorney on the other side.

Sir Thomas Farrer says a good deal about retaliation
—with a capital R—but I think my friend, the reasonable
reader, will at once see that there is no retaliation in the
matter.   Parrying a blow is not retaliation, though Sir
Thomas Farrer wishes us to believe that it is.   Protection
to foreigners on British markets is against our Free Trade
principles and contrary to justice and our own interests.
We therefore enter into a convention with certain countries
to secure the abolition of this protection.   But the foreign
Governments naturally point out that they cannot enter
into this arrangement unless they have some security that
they, in their turn, will not have to compete with bounty-
fed sugar.   It would be impossible to make a treaty without such security, and, as the object of the treaty is the
abolition of the most aggressive kind of protection, there
can be nothing of the nature of retaliation in giving the
required security in order to obtain a general agreement
for the abolition of the protection.   All this is so self-
evident that it seems almost ridiculous to state it in words,
and yet we are still met with the accusation of " trifling
with that two-edged weapon ' Retaliation.' "

Having started with the two fallacious assumptions, that bounties are good for us because they give us cheap sugar, and that their abolition involves " Protection " and " Retaliation " (the capitals are not mine), Sir Thomas Farrer makes the most of them in every by-path he can possibly discover. The " jam argument " was regarded by the Board of Trade for years as a splendid red herring to distract attention from the real facts of the sugar question, and Sir Thomas Farrer still shows how well this telling point can be brought in. A moment's reflection suffices to show how absolutely baseless it is. According to Sir Thomas Farrer's argument, if it means anything, the jam, confectionery, and biscuit trades were created by means of bounty-fed sugar, and depend for their existence on its maintenance. If it does not mean that, it means nothing, and yet it is only necessary to put it in those words in order to show its absurdity. The facts are that just as much jam, confectionery, and biscuits were made (per head of the population) when sugar was double the price. This is easily proved by the annual consumption of sugar, which shows no more rapid increase now than it did then. There could not be a more conclusive proof of the entire absence of any foundation for the " jam argument," with all its ornamental accessories of the enormous quantity of sugar required and number of men employed by these industries, all depending for their very existence on the maintenance of bounties. As Sir Thomas Farrer puts it, with earnest solemnity, " Are these industries which ought to be trifled with ? "

Another assumption, equally astounding when put in plain language, is that if we abolish bounties, " we put a stop to those manufactures of our own which we now export in order to pay for the bounty-fed sugar." This, if it means anything, must mean that whatever bounty-

fed sugar is used in this country is used over and above the
quantity which under normal conditions would be consumed. Thus stated, the point requires no further refutation; but if proof is required it may be found in the
statistics of our annual consumption to which I have
already referred. Sir Thomas Farrer will, no doubt, reply
that he did not say that this would be the result of
abolishing bounties, but of prohibiting them. But when
he wrote the sentence from which I have quoted he over-
looked what I had pointed out in reference to his former
letter, that, as the visible production of the world is five
million tons per annum, we shall continue to import whatever sugar we may want at the price ruling throughout
the world, whatever may happen with regard to the
remnant of bounty-fed sugar. Our consumers will continue to eat as much sugar, and therefore as much of our
own manufactures will continue to be exported in exchange
for it.

If I were not replying to letters which have been
characterised as "weighty" by very high authority, I
should feel constrained to apologise for wasting your
valuable space in refuting such glaring fallacies.

Among more miscellaneous errors, which I will correct
as briefly as possible, we come first to a repetition of what
I had already met in my former letter, that the bounties
are impossible to estimate. I will give one instance in
disproof of this. France, in 1884, started a new bounty
on production. This was done intentionally, not acci-
dentally, as Sir Thomas Farrer asserts, and it is this, not
the German bounty, as Sir Thomas Farrer says, which far
eclipses all other bounties. Part of the system is that the
French colonies shall receive exactly the same bounty as the
mother country, and this is accomplished by ascertaining
to a franc the amount of bounty obtained each year in the

French beetroot factories per 100 kilos of sugar, and giving exactly the same amount per 100 kilos to the French colonial sugar during the following year. What can be done in France can, of course, be done equally well elsewhere, the only data necessary for the calculation being the rate of duty and the yield of sugar. This is quite as accurately determined in Germany as in France.

On the point of cheapness, with which I have fully dealt, Sir Thomas Farrer makes a remark which is probably regarded as telling and unanswerable. He says producers are in a dilemma; the abolition of bounties will either make sugar dearer, or it will not; and if not, it will be of no benefit to them. This I have already met in my general argument as to cheapness. It is only occasionally, and for very short periods, that the competition forces prices down to a point at which producers lose, though with regard to refiners the process is a continuous one. The other influences brought about by bounties all tend to raise prices so far as production is concerned, consumers becoming more dependent every year on one particular crop; and as regards refined sugar, the cheapness is too small to be appreciable. It is the hindrance to progress and improvement and to the extension of cultivation which harasses producers quite as much as occasional depressions in the market, and it is for these reasons that they desire to be placed on equal terms with their competitors, if the mere fact of the inequality is not sufficient ground in itself for demanding abolition of bounties as a constitutional right.

In the effort to lay as much stress as possible on the word "cheap," Sir Thomas Farrer describes our sugar as so cheap that it is actually only half the price paid in the country of production. This is an absolute delusion. The price of sugar is the same all over the world; the on'y reason why it is dearer in some countries than in others is that in some it pays no duty, in others a low one, and in others a high one.

Sir Thomas Farrer asks, if we are going to abolish the sugar bounties, what are we going to do about shipping and other bounties? The answer is very simple. Do away with them if you can, in the interests of Free Trade.

The Board of Trade, he says, has enunciated the salutary doctrine that "Government should not interfere with the course of trade." Certainly, let us apply it to the case of the sugar bounties. The foreign Government interferes with the course of trade by giving bounties. If this interference operated only in its own country, we should have no right to meddle with the matter; but as the effect is to interfere very seriously with the course of trade in this country by actually handicapping British producers and manufacturers in their own home markets, those producers appeal to the very principle laid down by the Board of Trade.

It is quite right that our Government should not interfere with the course—the natural course—of trade. How much more true must this be, and how much more strictly should the principle be enforced, when we come to the extraordinary instance of a foreign Government interfering with the natural course of trade in British markets! And yet, when the very natural method of putting a stop to so flagrant a violation of Sir Thomas Farrer's principle by friendly international agreement is attempted, he resists it tooth and nail; first in the Board of Trade, then by leaflets of the Cobden Club, and lastly in four columns of *The Times*. "Let foreign nations take care of themselves," he says; "do not teach them that we are afraid of free imports." In this case the foreign nation is taking care of itself by handicapping British producers in their own markets, and Sir Thomas Farrer defends the process on principles of freedom and equality. Thus, the deeper we dig into his letters the further we get into the region of topsy-turvy. As in many other cases, Sir Thomas Farrer repeats a point which I had already fully met, without taking any notice of my remarks. "If it is right," he repeats, "to retaliate on bounties, it is much more right to retaliate on protective duties." The error here is threefold. In the first place, as I have shown, the action as to bounties cannot by any straining of terms be called retaliation. Secondly, the conditions are entirely different. Bounties operate aggressively by protecting foreign producers in this country, whereas foreign protective duties are an internal arrangement of the foreign country with which we have no right to interfere. Thirdly, any attempt to interfere with foreign protective duties by retaliation would in nearly all cases prove futile, while the very act of levying the retaliatory duty would create the very protection which I entirely agree with Sir Thomas Farrer in condemning. But in dealing with the bounty the process is exactly the reverse. The protection takes place in our market by the action of the foreigner. The removal or prohibition of the bounty annuls the protection, and restores Free Trade. The process is easy, effectual, and, in fact, the only way of securing a return to the condition of free imports which Sir Thomas Farrer so much desires, but will not permit. In fact, it is he who has perpetrated "the first official abandonment of that policy of free imports which has done so much for the material welfare of our toiling millions."

On all points I have now, as in times past, met Sir Thomas Farrer on his own ground, "the paramount interest of the consumer," and I therefore trust that if he continues his crusade in favour of bounties, he will first deal with my arguments thoroughly and in as straight-forward a way as I have endeavoured to demolish his. The question of the rights of the producer, whether master or man, I have hardly touched; but I should think that a good deal might be said about British producers—masters and men—having a constitutional right to demand equality with the foreigner on their own markets. At present the foreigner decrees that British producers of sugar shall not sell their goods under natural conditions in their own markets. They are to submit to be handicapped even in their own country. This is what Sir Thomas Farrer defends on Free Trade principles, and the Cobden Club backs him up. It is probably the most remarkable instance of science turned upside down that was ever seen.

Mr. Gladstone has called public attention to Sir Thomas Farrer's arguments as being "weighty." They have now in your columns been thoroughly weighed and found wanting. And yet no one could be found more capable than Mr. Gladstone, in his scientific days, to test the weight of arguments and facts. I cannot believe that, even if our sugar question were unfortunately to be dragged into the arena of party strife, the delicate balances so often used by our former chief would be found to have lost their accuracy.

CHAPTER III.

REPLY TO THE THIRD LETTER.

Sir,—At last Sir Thomas Farrer has replied to the arguments and facts by which we have traversed his original statements. Fortunately his reply is brief, so we can now bring the issue to a point. He does not, he says, maintain that bounties are making sugar cheaper, but he sticks to it that their abolition will make it dearer. In support of this paradox he cites, as usual, a memorandum of the Board of Trade which asserts that even the countervailing of the bounty would raise the price of sugar by a sum equal to a 2d. income tax. As we have already shown that even if bounty-fed sugar were prohibited prices would not be in any way affected, and as Sir Thomas Farrer has not dealt with our argument, it does not appear how quotations from his own memorandums strengthen his position. This is followed by a denial that the artificial stimulus to the production of beetroot sugar hinders progress in the production of cane sugar, and thereby makes the consumer every year more dependent on the beetroot crop. He supports this denial by quoting a Board of Trade report on the progress of the sugar trade. Well, all I can say is that we who pass our lives in the sugar market, and learn every fact respecting it with microscopic accuracy, are almost as good judges on this matter as the Board of Trade, which gets its information second-hand. In any case, I defy any statistics to disprove the simple fact that the increase in the world's consumption is being supplied by bounty-fed beetroot sugar.

The rest of Sir Thomas Farrer's reply is merely a re-assertion of statements, not a dealing with our refutation of them.

C

18

CHAPTER IV.

REPLY TO THE FOURTH LETTER.

Sir Thomas Farrer asks me to reply to four questions, all of which are so fully answered in my former letters that I almost fear he has not devoted such careful study to my arguments as I have to his. The questions to which he challenges me to reply can only be answered by repeating in brief what I have already argued in full. Sugar producers suffer from bounties quite as much by being deterred from progress as by being undersold. The amount by which refiners are undersold is too small to have any appreciable effect on prices. These points are fully explained in my letter of the 5th inst.

The exclusion of bounty-fed sugar would have the effect of immediately abolishing the bounty. As we have constantly explained, it is solely for the purpose of giving security to the contracting Powers and bringing about a general abolition of bounties that this penal clause is required, and is, in fact, indispensable. The industry has never asked for "the exclusion of foreign bounty-fed sugar to benefit our own sugar producers." We have argued in favour of a penal clause only because the negotiations for the suppression of bounties cannot be successful without it, and we have shown, as the *Spectator* puts it, that such a clause "is not only consistent with Free Trade, but positively conceived in the interests of Free Trade."

Sir Thomas Farrer's third question is best answered by transcribing it. "If bounty-fed sugar is the only source of supply from which the enormously increasing demand of the world is being met, and we cut off that supply, how can we do so without obliging people to use less sugar, or to pay more for it than they would do if that supply were not cut off?" The answer is so evident that it is almost unnecessary to formulate it. It is the bounty we wish to cut off, not the supply of sugar. We wish to bring back the production and manufacture of sugar into natural conditions—in other words to restore Free Trade—and we are bold enough, in our faith in Free Trade, to believe that under natural conditions sugar will be produced in sufficient quantities to supply all the wants of the world, and at the very lowest price at which its production and manufacture can be carried on. If Sir Thomas Farrer, as a political economist, objects to that arrangement, he must object to it on Protectionist, not on Free Trade grounds.

CHAPTER V.

REPLY TO THE SIXTH LETTER[*]

SIR,—Sir Thomas Farrer's attack on Baron de Worms must necessarily be a one-sided affair, it being evident that the Baron is not likely to enter into a newspaper controversy. It is clear that Sir Thomas Farrer has not read the speech he criticises, but only a summary. If he had he would have found that most of his points were fully met, and his questions answered. The occasion has, however, given him the opportunity of marshalling once more the dry bones of an army which has been cut to pieces long since. He had previously done his best to make your readers believe that the Convention is a Protectionist measure, and that it will make sugar dearer, and we had shown, in reply, that it is a Free Trade measure which will have no appreciable effect on the price of sugar, while it will free the consumer from his present dangerous position of dependence on an artificially stimulated source of production. Nevertheless, Sir Thomas Farrer reproduces the old phrases about Protection and dear sugar, just as if he had remained master of the situation, and his assertions had never been refuted.

In one place in the new letter Sir Thomas Farrer thinks that the abolition of bounties must cause a large rise in the price of sugar; in another he doubts whether bounties have had much to do with the cheapness of sugar. If this second view be correct, all his former energy in endeavouring to rescue the unfortunate consumer and jam maker from the

---

[*] Letter V., entitled "The Protocols," must be answered by a diplomatist.

danger of having bounties abolished was misdirected. If
the other be the true opinion it is clear that bounties ought
to have been abolished long ago, and before they had
brought about such a dependence on an artificial industry
that their removal involves scarcity and high prices.

In another place Sir Thomas Farrer says :—" My own
opinion has hitherto been that the effect of bounties is
much exaggerated, and that neither their continuance nor
their abolition would, in the face of more important factors,
have the effect attributed to them by the anti-bounty
agitators." He surely means "by Sir Thomas Farrer." It
is he only who has attributed effects of an exaggerated
character to the continuance or abolition of bounties. We
have confined ourselves to the modest statement that
bounty-fed competition robs us of our legitimate profit,
which may be represented by the small sum of 6d. per cwt.,
and has enabled foreign producers to be protected on British
markets to the extent of 350,000 tons of foreign refined
sugar per annum. As to the abolition of bounties, we have
simply pointed out that it would restore Free Trade, and
consequently benefit the consumer. The exaggerated
statements to which Sir Thomas Farrer refers are entirely
of his own invention ; such, for instance, as that the abolition
of bounties would deprive the jam and confectionery
makers of the bounty-fed sugar on which they depend for
their very existence. He now distinctly withdraws all that
part of his case by saying :—" As at present advised I doubt
whether bounties have had the effect attributed to them,
whether they constitute the chief causes of the recent cheapness of sugar." It is really time that Sir Thomas Farrer, if
he writes many more letters, should inform his readers who
these "anti-bounty agitators" are to whom he so repeatedly
refers, and what the exaggerated statements are which he
ascribes to them. After the careful and complete refutation

which we have given of the constantly reiterated assertions
of Sir Thomas Farrer, it is almost trifling with the subject
for him now calmly to ascribe them to "the anti-bounty
agitators." But he goes on to deal with Baron de Worms'
reply, that the abolition of bounties will not make sugar
dearer, and accepts it as probably correct. "But then," he
asks, "what becomes of the argument that it is the bounties
which have made sugar cheap, and have thus, as is alleged,
ruined our own sugar producers?" What, indeed? It is
one entirely of Sir Thomas Farrer's creation, and he seems,
at present, loth to part with it, though it has for some time
been in a ragged state.

Having at last come definitely to the conclusion that
the continuance of the bounties will not make sugar cheaper,
and that their abolition will not make it dearer, which, if
he had stated it earlier, would have saved us and your
readers a deal of trouble, Sir Thomas Farrer wavers and is
staggered by being told by Baron de Worms that the
European bounties amount to about £9,000,000 a year.
As the Board of Trade took the sugar question in hand
some years ago, it is difficult to understand why Sir Thomas
Farrer should be surprised at figures with which he ought
to be familiar. He thinks they show that the abolition of
bounties must cause a large rise in the price of sugar. If
so, they also show what a terrible rod in pickle the consumer
has laid up for himself by enjoying for so long the imaginary
benefits of bounty-fed sugar, and how much the Board of
Trade is to blame for resisting every effort to abolish
bounties at a time when their abolition would have had a
much less serious effect. A few years ago the consumer
was only dependent on bounty-fed sources of supply to the
extent of one-fifth of the world's visible production ; now
he is dependent on them to the extent of three-fifths of
the world's supply. It is therefore clear that if the abolition

of bounties is to raise prices—which it can only do by reducing production—it would do so much more violently
now than it would have done a few years ago. As long as
the bounties continue, the proportion of bounty-fed sugar
to the total supply of the world will constantly increase,
and consequently the longer we delay their abolition the
greater will be the danger and ultimate injury to the
consumer.

But Sir Thomas Farrer forgets that these bounties are
enabling an inferior article, beetroot, to compete with a
superior article, sugar-cane. The "gigantic subsidy"
which staggers him goes to make up the difference.
Cane sugar has not been ruined, as Sir Thomas Farrer
pretends. The industry can produce sugar at present
prices, and continues to do so, but it cannot progress in the
way it would have done if there had been free trade in
sugar. Planters and manufacturers are not disposed to
put fresh land into cultivation, erect new machinery, and
launch out into all the latest improvements, so long as the
present artificial state of things keeps matters in suspense
and destroys all confidence in the future.

At the outset of his letter Sir Thomas Farrer recapitu-
lates eleven points, which he says Baron de Worms has
failed to meet, any one of which is, in his opinion, enough
to destroy the Convention. I hope the readers of the
Times will not accept all such statements as true because
Sir Thomas Farrer declares them to be so. Nor can we
be expected to deal with all such statements of opinion—
the task would be endless. But when Sir Thomas Farrer
peruses the speech he will find that Baron de Worms dealt
with most of his eleven points, and saved the Convention
from immediate destruction. The large number of non-
contracting Powers is a pure assumption which has already
been shown to be entirely unfounded. The alleged breach

of commercial treaties is a matter which has been dealt
with very fully, and it has been urged at the Conferences,
as I pointed out before, that it is the bounties that are a
breach of commercial treaties. Sir Thomas Farrer comes
out now as a champion of Protection, for he actually
complains that the provisions of the Convention prevent us
from giving to our colonies the protection which the other
countries give to theirs. This objection is, in Sir Thomas
Farrer's opinion, enough to destroy the Convention, so he
evidently thinks that the country is going to take a new
departure in commercial policy, and condemns Baron de
Worms for sticking by the good old principle of Free
Trade. He conjures up a number of purely imaginary
objections to the Commission for carrying out the provisions of the treaty. They are absolutely groundless, and
yet he considers each one of them sufficient to destroy
the Convention. The old question of certificates of origin
was got rid of years ago, yet it now reappears as one of
the fatal objections. There are, according to Sir Thomas
Farrer, many other bounty-fed articles. We should be
glad to know of them, as they would be valuable allies, if
only in assisting us to meet his frequent onslaughts. The
Convention, it seems, is establishing a precedent which
will naturally lead to retaliation upon foreign corn. This
is one of the assertions which readers must not accept
merely because Sir Thomas Farrer happens to believe it.
We have already dealt fully with his use of the word
retaliation, and need not repeat the argument. It appears
that the one object which the authors of the Convention
have in view is the protection of our sugar industries ; and
yet we have fully explained that the only object is the
removal of protection to foreigners on British markets.

In joining issue with Baron de Worms on two points
Sir Thomas Farrer accepts his figures provisionally, and

only for the purpose of argument. But surely, figures are either right or wrong, and if wrong, any argument founded on them must be perfectly useless and mere waste of time. Sir Thomas Farrer does not deal with the correctness of the figures, but tries to throw discredit on them in this indirect way. The first of the two points which are thus argued is disposed of by the assertion that "if we cut off half the producing world from our market, we do not know how much sugar we may be excluding." Well, I should have thought we did know exactly. If we cut off half, surely we shall be excluding half. Although the idea is absurd, yet I am prepared to argue that even in that case we should still be buying sugar at the price ruling throughout the world, and that we should get as much sugar as we wanted. But I do not think that this ridiculous statement will mislead many of your readers. It is pretty well understood by this time that the penal clause is intended as a security to the contracting Powers, that the necessity for enforcing it is not likely to arise, and that if it were enforced it would at once bring about the abolition of the offending bounty ; and that even if it did not, it could not have any effect on the price of sugar throughout the world. The details of his argument are too far-fetched to be worth answering. I should advise Sir Thomas Farrer to investigate more minutely the Brazilian guarantee, and the sugar industry of the United States, before constructing further fancy fluctuations in the supply of sugar, and evolving the alarming situation on which he supports his phantom argument. It would be well to know something of the rudiments of the subject before instructing the public through your valuable columns on the details of an imaginary sugar trade. Sir Thomas Farrer is rapidly developing into a commercial Rider Haggard.

The second point on which a reply is given to Baron

de Worms is the cheap sugar question, with which I have already dealt, and which is now settled in my favour.

There remains only the peroration, in which Sir Thomas Farrer regrets that this country has not waited quietly until the bounties are abolished spontaneously, and gives as his reason the very fact which has brought about the present international arrangement. Germany and Austria wished to get rid of bounties, but unfortunately France, jealous of the success of the German and Austrian industries, started the same fiscal system, but on a very exaggerated scale. It became absolutely necessary to do something to check such a monster bounty, and consequently the other countries were not sorry to see Great Britain make a proposal for united action. How Sir Thomas Farrer can point to this situation as an argument for doing nothing it is difficult to understand.

Your readers will begin to ask why there should be all this volume of controversy. We have also wondered to the same effect. But still the nice long columns of nice large print, in Sir Thomas Farrer's pleasant readable style, continue to appear at regular intervals. What is it all about? Why this persistent assertion of that which has been shown to be erroneous? Why should the protection of foreigners on British markets be so constantly and vigorously defended by an undoubted Free Trader?

The letter concludes with a handsome apology to Baron de Worms, thoroughly spoiled by the very gratuitous remark that his action can only be accounted for by the fact that he is a sincere and deep, even if unadmitted and unconscious Protectionist. It is necessary to bring that word in prominently, though Sir Thomas Farrer knows perfectly well that abolition of bounties is a restoration of Free Trade.

As Baron de Worms is unable to reply in your

columns, I hope you will permit me to do so, and I urge
my request on the further strong ground that Sir Thomas
Farrer does not hesitate to repeat assertions without
attempting to meet the arguments by which we have
refuted them.

CHAPTER VI.

REPLY TO A LETTER WHICH IS NOT REPRODUCED.

SIR,—You say to-day, in reference to another matter, "great is the power of undaunted assertion." In the wielding of this power Sir Thomas Farrer has for years been an eminent expert, and he exercises it once more, I hope for the last time, in his reply* to the arguments I have ventured to put forward in refutation of his statements. He will not attempt, he says, to reply at length, as it would involve a repetition of former arguments. But how can a refutation be met by a repetition of the statements it professes to refute? I may, therefore, fairly assume that my arguments are unanswerable, except as regards the "one or two points" which Sir Thomas Farrer considers to require further notice. Let us see what they amount to.

Sir Thomas Farrer again urges the point that foreign protective duties interfere as much with the freedom of trade as bounties. I dealt fully with this point, but Sir Thomas refers to only a portion of my argument, and in doing so he is obliged to use, as his only rejoinder, the assertion that bounties do us more good than harm. As a great portion of my former letters was directed to show that this is an entirely erroneous assumption, and that, on the contrary, bounties are an injury to the consumer as well as to the producer, it is hardly fair fighting to decline to meet the arguments I adduced in refutation of the assertion, and then to repeat it as a rejoinder on another point.

* Dated October 24th.

My argument, if I recollect right, was that if we were to retaliate against foreign protective duties we should be attacking foreign Governments with regard to a matter in which they are entirely within their rights, namely, their own import duties. We should, moreover, be rushing into Protection and injuring our consumers for a very problematical benefit. On the other hand, any course we may pursue for the abolition of bounties would be carried out without recourse to retaliation, it would be reasonable and desirable as a means of removing the most flagrant instance of Protection which it is possible to imagine, namely, the protection of foreigners on British markets, and its only result would be the restoration of Free Trade by the removal of the bounty. This restoration of Free Trade is as necessary for the consumer as for the producer, since he would otherwise become more and more dependent every year on the artificial source of production.

The other point to which Sir Thomas Farrer returns affords me the very best means of illustrating the false position into which the consumer is brought by the operation of bounties. He thinks I have not sufficiently answered his argument, that if the increase in the world's consumption is met by bounty-fed sugar, and we cut off that supply, we must either reduce consumption or increase the price. My reply was to the effect that the operation of the Convention would be to abolish bounties, and that if Sir Thomas Farrer feared that one or two countries might still remain obstinate and continue to give bounties—a very improbable supposition—the annual available production of the world, five million tons, would be sufficient to keep up our supply at the world's price, whatever it might be. I admit that, when I stated that argument in reply to Sir Thomas Farrer, I did not by any means exhaust the subject. I did not, for instance, meet the supposition that a

cutting-off of the bounty might involve a cutting-off of the
supply of sugar which we now get from bounty-fed sources.
That may be a supposition within the bounds of possibility,
and if that is what is in the mind of Sir Thomas Farrer, it
furnishes me with a most splendid illustration of the injury
which is being inflicted on British consumers by foreign
bounties. Of the five million tons which constitute the
world's visible and available annual supply of sugar, more
than half consists of beetroot sugar, nearly all of which is
bounty-fed. If the abolition of the bounties means the
" cutting-off" of this supply, the unfortunate consumer will,
indeed, have to pay dearly for the privilege of eating
bounty-fed sugar. If this is to be the result, would it not
have been better for Sir Thomas Farrer and the Board of
Trade to have permitted the abolition of bounties ten years
ago, when the effect would have been less severe ; or would
it not be better to do so even now, rather than wait till
beetroot sugar grows to still larger proportions, and the
consumer runs the risk of a still more serious famine when
things are at last righted, as they certainly will be some
day ? As I said before, I fear no such result from
the abolition of bounties. They have, it is true, helped
greatly in establishing a most important industry on the
Continent, but I fully believe that, when the bounties are
abolished, that industry will enter heartily upon a Free
Trade struggle with cane sugar. Our colonial producers
are quite aware of this, and neither they nor ourselves
shrink from the contest. We and our colonial friends
have hitherto had to contend against beetroot plus bounties.
Remove the bounties, and we are ready to hail the beetroot in the same kindly spirit that we regard any fair and
equal competition, from whatever part of the world it may
come.

I am, of course, glad that Sir Thomas Farrer has not

attempted any serious reply to my arguments. We may congratulate ourselves that two facts in connection with bounties are now fully established ; they are no benefit to us whether we be consumers or producers, and their abolition is essentially a Free Trade measure.

It is to be hoped that the absurdly exaggerated misconceptions with regard to this matter, of which we have read so much during the last few weeks, will now give place to more rational views. The subject, from the consumer's point of view, is of much greater importance, and involves considerations which go much deeper down into the region of first principles than the general public are at present aware. It is also a colonial question of very great interest, and one not confined alone to our West Indian colonies. I hope, therefore, that it will continue to meet with proper attention from public men, quite apart from the sugar refiner's position, and I earnestly trust that it will be dealt with on its merits, and not as merely furnishing clap-trap for political speeches.

CHAPTER VII.

REPLY TO THE FIRST REJECTED LETTER.

SIR THOMAS FARRER regrets, with regard to Mr. Goschen, "the great amount of human sacrifice which the exigencies of our politics demand." In other words, he regrets that Mr. Goschen has changed his views about Free Trade because he is a member of Her Majesty's Government. Without commenting on the good taste of this insinuation, in reference to a matter which, but for Sir Thomas Farrer, would be quite outside party politics, it may be asked what evidence there is that Mr. Goschen has not always held the same views which he is now prepared to defend. It is well known that many eminent Free Traders have defended the policy of the Convention, as "not only consistent with Free Trade, but positively conceived in the interests of Free Trade." There is, therefore, no reason to brand Mr. Goschen as an apostate, or to ascribe to him unworthy political motives, because he is of the same opinion. However, he will no doubt defend himself against this gratuitous attack at the proper time.

The resolutions of Trades Unions, representing nearly half a million of the working classes, expressing satisfaction with the penal clause of the Convention, are regarded by Sir Thomas Farrer as hopelessly at variance with the terms of the Convention. His first reason for this opinion, a most curious and inconclusive one, is that the Protocol has not been signed by the United States, a country which naturally did not sign, as it did not send delegates to the Conference. The reservations of other States, on which he lays stress, had nothing to do with the penal clause;

and France, which he especially names, took a leading
part in its introduction. The second reason—namely, that
the clause excludes the whole product—is eminently un-
reasonable, because it must be evident that if security is
to be given to the contracting Powers by this mutual
engagement, it must be by dealing with the sugar production of a bounty-giving country as a whole.

The observations in reference to the history of the
penal clause are quite inaccurate. The proposal is in no
way adverse to the interest of England as a consuming
nation, as we have frequently pointed out in our replies
to Sir Thomas Farrer's previous letters. But this is his
special method of controversy. He not only fails to deal
with replies to his arguments, but he takes every opportunity of repeating what has already been fully refuted
This country has the whole world open to it from which
to draw its supplies of sugar. Even if the product of one
particular country were shut out—a contingency which
would almost certainly never practically arise—the bulk
of the five million tons of the world's annual production
would still be free to enter British markets at the world's
price. The objects aimed at by Spain and Germany are
quite misrepresented. Spain's object was, like that of all
who desire the abolition of bounties, simply to restore
freedom of competition, and thus enable her colonial producers to progress under natural conditions, free from the
repressive influences of the bounty system. The object
of Germany was to stop the big bounty by means of which
the French hope to regain their ascendency in the beetroot industry. They both desire the penal clause, not for
the purpose, as Sir Thomas Farrer pretends, of keeping
sugar out of British markets, but as a mutual security
against protected competition. But these facts do not suit
Sir Thomas Farrer's line of thought, so they are twisted

D

into language which when examined proves to be incorrect. Spain and Germany know perfectly well that they cannot —though Sir Thomas Farrer puts the words into their mouth—raise their prices to the English consumer. Prices can only be raised by reducing production, and that certainly will not be the effect of abolishing bounties. If bounties be abolished, the production of cane sugar will undoubtedly be largely increased, and that of beetroot will certainly not fall off. The trade know perfectly well, whatever Sir Thomas Farrer may say to the contrary, that prices will not rise ; * but they also know that producers will at last be able to carry on their business with a sense of security to which they have long been strangers, and which the restoration of Free Trade in sugar can alone insure.

We now come to a very amusing episode in Sir Thomas Farrer's attack. In piteous terms he complains that in negotiating this Convention the Board of Trade was not consulted. What does this mean ? Was not Baron de Worms himself one of the chiefs of the Board of Trade, and was not that department also represented, and very ably represented, by Mr. Bateman ? But, remembering the evidence given before the Select Committee of the House of Commons by Board of Trade officials, it was not to be expected that that department would be asked to take the whole control of the matter. The views of the department were peculiar. They were strongly in favour of bounties, so much so in fact that they, or some of them, regarded a reduction of wages as a better remedy for the evils arising from bounties than the abolition of the bounties themselves. This was a strong view to take, and was naturally resented by the working-classes. An attempt

---

* *See* Appendix, page 138.

was made to deny that any such view had been propounded, but the evidence is too distinct to be got over. The Committee were naturally astonished at such a doctrine, and gave the witness every opportunity, in cross-examination, to explain it away, but each question only resulted in emphasising the original statement, and there is no context, in the rest of the evidence, to mitigate its effect. Here are the questions and answers, which, it must be remembered, were submitted to the witness for correction before being published :—

Report, Sugar Industries, August, 1880.

Minutes of Evidence, page 18, Question 283.

" Supposing pretty equal conditions, one man gets £2 a ton and the other gets nothing ; the man who gets nothing would hardly be able to compete with the man who gets the £2 a ton on an article of £22, would he ?—I do not know but what he might be able to do so, if he lowered the profits and wages in his trade. There are many conditions under which a great many people could compete. You might reduce the rent of a great deal of property which was growing cane sugar, so that you might have a large amount of competition still."

Page 28, Questions 469, 470.

" It is your opinion, in answer to Question 283, that export bounties must be met by a reduction of wages ?— Yes ; that was suggested in reply to a question which was put to me, and I said that when two men were competing, if one of them got a special advantage of that kind, it did not necessarily follow that the other man was put out of the trade, but that he might meet it by reducing his wages or profits."

" You think reducing the wages of the working men and keeping on the bounty is better than taking off the bounty and keeping the wages as they are ?—Yes."

The next statement of Sir Thomas Farrer's is entirely
erroneous. He says, that though the poor neglected
Board of Trade was not consulted, in spite of the
presence of its chief secretary as President of the Conference—a curious complaint for a subordinate official to make
with regard to his chief—yet the trades were no doubt
consulted, and the agitators were set in motion whilst the
public were kept in the dark. This most improper accusation is absolutely without foundation, and is exactly the
reverse of the facts, which are as follows :—A working man
of literary ability, quite unknown till the other day to anyone connected with sugar, was writing a series of able
articles in a provincial newspaper, and, among other subjects, dealt with the sugar question, about which he said
a good many things which were telling and some that were
unsound. But he wound up by declaring that working
men were not going to stand bounty-fed competition, and
that the way they meant to remedy it was to prohibit the
importation of bounty-fed sugar. This spontaneous,
individual opinion was the first that the sugar trade heard
about prohibition. The Trades Unions took up the idea,
and their action resulted in the resolutions to Lord
Salisbury from all the leading Trades Councils in the
kingdom. No idea then existed that any such proposal
was being considered at the Conference, and the first that
was heard of it was at a dinner given by the Grocers'
Company to the International Delegates, long after the
action of the Trades Councils. With the exception of the
hint given on that occasion, the trade were as ignorant as
the rest of the world of the stipulations of the Convention
until their publication.

This part of the subject winds up with a very undigni-
fied sneer at Baron de Worms, who is accused of comparing
himself, in his Greenock speech, with the great author of

the French Commercial Treaty. He does nothing of the kind. In reply to Sir Thomas Farrer's taunt about his going cap in hand to foreign Powers, Baron de Worms asks what there was exceptional in such a course. Did not Cobden go to Paris? Did not Mr. Chamberlain go to Washington? And this is what Sir Thomas Farrer calls "self-conscious pride in his own achievement," and so on. Baron de Worms was simply answering an argument, and justifying the action of the Government by quoting precedents. There is too much of personal spite appearing in Sir Thomas Farrer's unpublished letters. The earlier ones were not altogether free from it, but in these latter ones it is so offensively prominent as quite to justify the *Times* in suppressing them.

But this is not enough. In a footnote to this insult Sir Thomas Farrer tries to make out, because Baron de Worms quoted the Merchandise Marks Act in one of his speeches, that therefore it is he and not the Trades Councils who drew the parallel. Though this inference is unfounded, the point is quite immaterial, except that it contains an insinuation that the Trades Councils were prompted, which is not the case. The further suggestion, that the parallel between prohibiting fraudulent trade marks and prohibiting bounty-fed sugar is unsound, because in the first case the offender is treated as a criminal, is incorrect. The object of prohibiting fraudulent trade marks is not to punish the offender but to defend the trade of this country against unfair competition in its own markets, the very same object as that for which bounties are to be abolished.

The Trades Councils would not, in Sir Thomas Farrer's opinion, have adopted these resolutions if they had been acquainted with the facts of the case. These facts are, according to Sir Thomas Farrer, that under the present

régime of bounties, which he calls free imports, prices have
fallen to less than half of that which other countries have
to pay; that the Convention would diminish the supply
and raise the price; that it would, in fact, cut off half the
sources of our supply; that it endangers our trade; and
finally, that it leads the way "to protection of corn."
This gives an opportunity for Sir Thomas Farrer's glaring
fallacies, which have been refuted again and again, to be
once more marshalled in force, as if they had never been
defeated, or even attacked, and were invulnerable.   But he
certainly will not succeed in getting the leaders of the
working classes to be deceived by any such language.
Their brains are made of very different stuff from what he
imagines.   They are very quick to see the weak point of
an argument, and fortunately have plenty of good solid
common sense.   They know perfectly well that this
country buys sugar at the same price as the rest of the
world, and no cheaper; that the Convention will increase
our supplies and therefore lessen rather than increase the
price; that to talk about cutting off half our source of
supply is an insult to their common sense; that in all
probability the penal clause will never be enforced, but
that if it is it will be on such a small scale, as compared
with the production of the world, that it can have no
possible effect on our supply of sugar; that the danger to
our trade is a bogey conjured up by Sir Thomas Farrer
for the purpose of upsetting an arrangement about which
he peevishly complains that he was not consulted; and,
finally, that abolishing bounties has nothing whatever to do
with protecting corn.   They have not taken up the subject
for the reasons imagined by Sir Thomas Farrer, but for the
very simple one, so apparent to minds which prefer
straight to crooked ways, that they would not like to see
their own trade disturbed and harassed by foreign bounty-

fed competition. If Sir Thomas Farrer succeeds in throwing sufficient dust in the eyes of professional politicians to procure the defeat of the Convention, he will find that he has not won for himself the gratitude of the working classes; and he will then discover that this fear of the bounty system being extended to other trades will raise an outcry which no Government will be able to withstand. A proposal to neutralise the effect of bounties by reducing wages is bad enough, but a direct encouragement to foreign Powers to stimulate other trades by means of bounties will turn out to be even worse.

The letter ends with the usual little bit of party politics, which is quite beside the question except as indicating the animus of the writer.

The last words are a cry: " Free Imports and Cheap Food." That is exactly what those who advocate the abolition of bounties desire. At present the unsubsidised producer who desires to bring his sugar to this or any other country is not free to do so unless he is prepared to compete against those who receive a subsidy over and above their natural profit. This is not freedom, and it tends to discourage natural production, and to make the consumer dependent on the artificial sources of supply, a process which is not conducive to cheap food, and must inevitably result, if Free Trade be not restored, in dear food. It has been sufficiently often pointed out, in reply to Sir Thomas Farrer, that a refusal to abolish bounties means the maintenance of protection to foreigners on British markets, and such a diversion of the natural channels of supply as must eventually prove injurious to the interests of the consumer. Though this is one of the first principles of Free Trade, it is persistently ignored in Sir Thomas Farrer's book.

CHAPTER VIII.

REPLY TO THE SECOND REJECTED LETTER.

No wonder that *The Times* declined to insert this letter, for it is nothing but a *réchauffé*, almost in identical phrases, of the letters which had already appeared. To the contentions contained in it we have replied most conclusively and repeatedly in letters which have also been published in the columns of *The Times*, but to which Sir Thomas Farrer has never attempted to reply. He is trifling with the subject and his readers by constantly repeating what has already been so frequently and so fully refuted by facts and arguments which he has failed to meet.

Sir Thomas Farrer begins by citing various instances of supposed interference by foreign Governments with production, with the view of stimulating it, and asks whether these cases are to be dealt with on the same principles as the sugar bounties. That must depend on their nature and extent, and on the possibility of applying the same remedy, namely, international agreement. Some of his instances are very far fetched: Indian railways, for instance, enjoy a Government guarantee,* but it would be difficult to prove that that fact amounts to a bounty on the production of corn; certainly it does not constitute a

---

* The railways pay a higher dividend than that guaranteed by Government, so there is absolutely nothing in the point. The *Economist* says this is not so, but it turns out that this is a worse mistake than Sir Thomas Farrer's. I find on enquiry that out of a total of 781,088 tons of wheat exported from India in 1888, 631,811 tons were shipped from Bombay and Calcutta, and were conveyed to the ports of shipment by the East Indian, the Great Indian Peninsula, and the Bombay and Baroda Railway Companies—all companies earning more than the guaranteed dividend.

bounty on its exportation. Sir Thomas Farrer must be
hard up for arguments when he calls the repealing of an
export duty "favouring sugar," and actually quotes it as
one of his instances of bounties which have been over-
looked.

But the next instance is still more strange. He urges
that "every protective duty or surtax is a bounty on
export, since, by enabling the native producer to get a
high price at home, it enables and induces him to throw
his surplus on foreign markets at an unnaturally low
price." In other words, a foreign producer who has
realised and safely deposited at his bankers a large profit
on his home trade, is actually so foolish as to draw it out
of his bank and present it to consumers in this or other
countries in the form of goods at an unnaturally low
price. There is an excellent illustration in the sugar
trade to show how directly contrary to actual practice this
absurd theory is. The American refiners are highly protected in their own markets; not an ounce of foreign
refined is admitted. A short time ago they had a bounty
on export, and sent large quantities of refined sugar to this
country. The bounty was reduced to an amount which did
not enable them any longer to compete with the larger
bounties of Europe. Their exports immediately disappeared. Now, if Sir Thomas Farrer is right, they ought
to have gone on exporting, utilising the large profits made
in their protected home market to undersell foreigners
abroad. But, instead of that, they did exactly the reverse,
as any sensible man under the circumstances would do.
They took care never to make more than their home
market required, and the large profits which they consequently realise they are keeping in their own pockets, in
preference to distributing them philanthropically throughout the world.

As to the possibility of extending the bounty system to other trades, Sir Thomas Farrer, in the form of a question to Lord Salisbury, ridicules the idea that "intelligent Governments would, out of pure perversity, and at great loss to themselves, voluntarily continue to make, out of the money of their taxpayers, a present of the products of their industry to foreign nations." But, as it happens, this is exactly what France did in 1884. There was no bounty on beetroot sugar in France before that date. There had been a heavy bounty on refined, and the French beetroot sugar manufacturers co-operated heartily with the British sugar refiners in getting it greatly reduced. But when the German bounty grew to large dimensions, the French beetroot sugar manufacturers saw that they must also have a bounty if they were to maintain the competition. Hence the law of 1884, which deliberately gave to the French manufacturers a bounty which, according to the Minister of Finance, amounted one year to 92,000,000 francs. If the Government of one of the leading European nations—a Republican Government—takes such a deliberate step as this, and knowingly sacrifices such an enormous revenue, why should not a hundredth part of that vast sum be cheerfully voted as an export bounty on boots and shoes? Sir Thomas Farrer falls into his old error in calling an export bounty a gratuitous present to foreign nations. It is nothing of the kind. The exporter takes care to sell his wares at the full market value. It is only when the bounty has had the inevitable effect of over-stimulating production that the bounty-fed exporter begins to find that he must part with some of his artificial profit. But the portion which he gives away must always be very small, because he does not need to part with it until the level of cost price has been over-stepped, and directly that occurs competition ceases, and the bounty-fed producer has it all his

own way. The present made to foreign nations is, therefore, illusory, and for practical purposes non-existent.

Sir Thomas Farrer next asks Lord Salisbury "whether
as a matter of fact, notwithstanding the long existence of
sugar bounties, the production of sugar in all parts of the
world—bounty-fed or not bounty-fed—has not been constantly increasing?" Is this advanced as a reason against
abolishing bounties? Or is it regarded as strengthening
the position so persistently taken up by Sir Thomas
Farrer, in the face of overwhelming facts and arguments to
the contrary, that the abolition of bounties will make
sugar dearer? It is greatly to the credit of producers who
receive no bounties that, in spite of bounties which have
greatly assisted in the enormous increase in the production
of beetroot sugar, they have been able not only to hold
their own but to creep slowly ahead. There can be no
stronger proof of the correctness of the anticipation that
when bounties are abolished the production of cane sugar
will expand rapidly, and that consumers will thereby
secure a large increase in their supplies, an increase which
will not be dependent on the caprice of foreign Governments. The evil of the bounties has been that producers
never knew what was coming next. The rapid extension
of the beetroot crop under this artificial stimulus caused a
temporary glut in the markets of the world five years ago,
which was only remedied by the forcible contraction of
that crop, and by the accidental coincidence of an unpro-
pitious season. But so long as bounties continue there is
nothing to prevent and everything to encourage a periodical
recurrence of these unnatural gluts, which cause enormous
confusion, and often disaster, to the whole sugar trade of
the world, and certainly discourage any natural progress
and improvement outside the area of bounties. Hence the
whole trade becomes every year more and more at the

mercy of the European production, of the climatic influences over a comparatively small area of the sugar producing world, and of the constant changes in the bounty
system. All this disturbance to the natural course of trade
Sir Thomas Farrer desires to continue, and yet claims to
be the champion of Free Trade principles.

There are one or two points in explanation of the
present slight increase in the production of cane sugar
which are worth noting incidentally, as Sir Thomas
Farrer has raised the question, though they have nothing
to do with the subject of sugar bounties. For instance,
Australia has of late years become a large producer of
sugar, parts of Queensland being eminently suited to the
growth of the sugar-cane. It was quite possible, a few
years ago, for that large increase to take place at the other
side of the world, solely for the supply of the home consumption, even while European bounties were going on
increasing. But when the great glut of 1884 took place,
the Australians at once saw that even they were no longer
outside the influence of the sugar bounties; and since
then they have been as active as any in urging that some
means should be found for stopping so unnatural and
injurious a competition. Another instance of very large
increase in production is to be found in the Sandwich
Islands, but this is fully explained by the fact that they
have the peculiar advantage of being able to sell their
sugar in the United States at the duty-paid price without
having paid the duty. The answers to Sir Thomas
Farrer's questions to Lord Salisbury with regard to an
extension of the bounty system, and to the actual increase
in the production of sugar, are not, therefore, as he
assumes, calculated "to allay Lord Salisbury's appre-
hensions."

Sir Thomas Farrer passes to another subject, and states

that the Protectionist Party in the United States have
proposed a direct and intentional bounty on the export
of sugar, as a compensation to the sugar producers for
the proposed repeal of the duty. This is an error. It
has been proposed to halve the present duty on sugar;
and as the Louisiana planters at present enjoy the privilege of selling their sugar at the duty-paid price without
having paid any duty, it is clear that if the duty were
halved they would lose half their artificial profit. It has
been proposed to make this up to them by giving them in
cash about the same amount as they would lose. But
this is no more a bounty on export than their present
artificial profit is. They do not want an export bounty,
nor would they use it if they had it, seeing that they do not
produce one-tenth of the consumption of the United States.
Their whole advantage is derived from being able to sell
their sugar for home consumption without having paid any
duty on it. There is no drawback on the exportation of
it, and, moreover, even the refiners are compelled to make
a declaration that the sugar they export and receive drawback on is not made from duty-free sugar. Nothing could
prove more conclusively that the United States Government is determined that no bounty on export shall be
obtained, and the same determination is shown in the
wording of the law regulating the drawback on refined,
and also of the Bill to which Sir Thomas Farrer refers,
but which, apparently, he has not seen. He even makes
the further mistake of supposing that the proposed bounty
was also to be given on refining.

Now comes another repetition of old and exploded
ideas, which are found so telling to the ignorant and un-
suspicious reader that Sir Thomas Farrer loses no opportunity of repeating them, quite regardless of the refutations
which he has failed to combat. Bounties, he repeats, are

an interference with trade which does harm to the people
of the country which gives them, but good to us, " by giving
us cheap sugar at their expense." First, with regard to
the injury ascribed to bounties, it may be pointed out in
passing, without in any way defending the system, that
though it is a burden on the taxpayer, it certainly has, in
the case of Germany, assisted in building up one of the
finest industries in the world—an industry the benefits of
which are very widespread and far-reaching. Secondly, as
to its benefit to us, the contention of Sir Thomas Farrer
has been shown, over and over again, to be not only unfounded, but the reverse of the fact. He is, in fact, arguing
in favour of Protection when he argues this main point
of his whole contention, that a gross infraction of the first
principles of Free Trade—a diversion of the natural
channels of supply—is to be defended on the ground that
it is beneficial. He is wrong, therefore, in principle ; but
he is still more wrong in his facts. The bounties do not
give us cheap sugar. He uses the expression even more
incorrectly in some passages, where he refers to the cheap
bounty-fed sugar as distinguished from the dear sugar
which receives no bounty. There is no such thing as
cheap bounty-fed sugar, because all sugar is sold at the
same price—quality for quality—no matter what may be
its origin. Sir Thomas Farrer knows this perfectly well ;
if he does not, he is quite unfit to deal with this or any
other commercial question. The only way in which
bounties make sugar cheap is by stimulating production ;
but then they at the same time tend to make sugar dear
by discouraging production, so that their ultimate effect
must be to leave the consumer dependent on the bounty-
fed production, which is clearly a very undesirable position.
Then, again, the bounty-fed producer does not give a
farthing of his bounty to the consumer until cost price is

reached ; and directly you go below that point the bounty-
fed producer is master of the situation. This, again, is not
a desirable position for the consumer. Thus Sir Thomas
Farrer's benefit derived from bounties, which he is so
anxious to retain, turns out to be no benefit, but an injury.

Bounties should therefore be abolished. Foreign Governments have at last expressed their readiness to abolish
them, if possible, by mutual agreement. But one thing is
absolutely essential to such an agreement; there must be
some security that it will be loyally carried out, and that
the contracting Powers will be free from bounty-fed competition in the future. Hence the penal clause. There was
no other way in which an agreement could be brought
about. The principle was admitted in the old Convention
of 1864, and was objected to by no one. The many International Conferences which have been held since then have
clearly proved that no progress could be made till the contracting Powers were furnished with the necessary security
against bounty-fed competition. The principle of such a
clause has been declared by many high authorities of all
shades of political opinion to be perfectly sound, and the
clause to be absolutely necessary for the restoration of Free
Trade. But, unfortunately, Sir Thomas Farrer thought
otherwise, and his department consequently barred all progress for many years. At last Lord Salisbury's Government
thought fit to override the views of the Board of Trade, and
hence Sir Thomas Farrer's tears. Hence it is that he over-
strains his argument and tries to make out that the penal
clause will strike half the sugar of the world, whereas it will
probably never strike an ounce. He assumes that " jealous
rivals " will search the by-paths of the world for petty
bounties, in order that the penal clause may not remain a
dead letter. All this is the discontented resentment of an
official who thinks his opinion has been slighted. The real

fact being that if his erroneous views had been overruled
some years ago, great trouble and havoc in the sugar
market would have been prevented, and we should by this
time have been enjoying the blessings of Free Trade.

He objects to thus bringing about an agreement for the
abolition of bounties, for the same reason that he objects to
a protective duty on foreign corn. He goes further, and
says that all Free-traders object for that reason, whereas
in point of fact many Free-traders do not object but
approve, and certainly no Free-trader in his senses would
object for such a reason as that. There is no parallel in
any way between the two cases. A protective duty on
corn means, first, that the consumer has to pay an extra
price equal to the amount of the duty ; and secondly, that
the home-producer receives an artificial profit equal to the
amount of the duty. On the other hand, the penal clause
of the Convention cannot, under any circumstances, prevent
the British consumer from obtaining as much sugar as he
can possibly require out of the five million tons of the
world's annual production, at the free and open price ruling
throughout the world, without hindrance or duty of any
kind. The consumer has not, therefore, as in the former
case, to pay any extra price, nor does the home or colonial
producer receive any artificial profit. And yet Sir Thomas
Farrer does not hesitate even to go so far, in throwing dust
in the eyes of his readers, as to pretend that the penal
clause will limit the supply of sugar and thereby make it
dearer. The fact that there are five million tons to choose
from is a sufficient refutation of this deliberate attempt to
deceive ; but there is a better refutation in Sir Thomas
Farrer's own words. Speaking farther on, at page 69, of
French sugar going to the United States and turning out
West India sugar, he concludes :—"And then the only
effect of the Convention, so far as British interests are

concerned, will be to divert good and cheap beet-sugar from
the United Kingdom to the United States, to give us bad
West India sugar instead of good beet-sugar, and, as
regards the West Indies, to give them a market here, but
at the same time to deprive them of a market in America,
which is at least equally good." Quite so; when Sir
Thomas Farrer got as far as page 69, he found out that the
only operation of the penal clause, at the very worst, would
be to substitute one sugar for another; but here, at page
51, and in many other places, he does not hesitate to stick
to his old fallacy, which sounded so telling and conclusive,
and so destructive to the policy of the Convention, and to
continue to assert, in direct contradiction to his own deliberate statements elsewhere, that the result of the Convention must be to restrict supply and make sugar dearer. It
is a shame that those who desire the success of the Convention should be compelled to deal with such glaring cases of
deliberate misstatement. But look at the language of the
passage quoted above: "Good and cheap beet-sugar" is
a curious expression in many ways; so is "bad West India
sugar." Many people prefer cane sugar to beetroot, some
even go so far as to give a higher price for it. Sir Thomas
Farrer is not one of these; in fact, his language would
almost lead to the inference that he was a partisan of the
beetroot industry. But according to his view, beetroot is
not only "good" but "cheap." The sugar market is evidently governed by some new economical law, not previously discovered, which causes the good article to fetch
less money than the bad. As to West India sugar being
"bad," Sir Thomas Farrer would find plenty of people in
Mincing Lane, both refiners and dealers, who would be
thankful for such a good supply of fine West India sugar
as used to come to market twenty years ago.

This enormous fallacy leads on to others. The

E

imaginary restriction of supply, as stated at page 51, and shown to be impossible at page 69, must involve a curtailment or destruction of "the work of those who make the goods with which we pay for foreign sugar." So that at page 51 Sir Thomas Farrer seriously believes that, in spite of there being every year five million tons of sugar to choose from, we are to be subject to a positive famine because, by the possible operation of the penal clause, the quantity of the world's production which will remain free to enter British markets may be reduced to 4,950,000 tons, or any other figure he likes to imagine. He fails to see that the balance goes on to do its part in keeping down the world's price, and that the world's price will always be our price. We shall, therefore, have the same quantity of sugar at the same price whether the penal clause is enforced or not. The people who make goods to pay for sugar will not, therefore, be ruined by a sugar famine, nor will the jam-makers suddenly find their raw material cut off. The beautiful structure so carefully raised on no foundation goes to pieces, and the vigorous conclusion of the argument, namely, that Lord Salisbury is sacrificing "the whole to a class, the many to the few," which is "the very essence of Protection," falls to the ground, it is to be hoped for the last time. The abolition of bounties, as has now been repeatedly shown in reply to these clap-trap assertions, is necessary, not for the benefit of or even in justice to the few, but for the welfare of the whole community, since bounties tend to contract supplies within an artificial area, and must eventually leave the consumer at the mercy of a protected monopoly. The attempt to remedy this flagrant breach of the first principles of Free Trade is condemned by Sir Thomas Farrer because he happens to have made a mistake and does not like to admit it ; he, therefore, sticks to it that it is "the very essence of Protection."

This is followed by another repetition—the whole book is a series of repetitions, one tune without even the relief of variations—of the statement that a large proportion of the sugar of the world is to be excluded. This is absolutely untrue and impossible. The worst that could happen is that France should continue to give her large bounty, and refuse to join the Convention. Sir Thomas Farrer takes care not to tell his readers how small a proportion of our imports comes from France. But whether the proportion were large or small it would not matter, as has been repeatedly explained. We can get any quantity of sugar at the world's price, whether France be shut out or not. France sends us only refined sugar, and the market quotations show that the trade, and therefore the consumers, greatly prefer British refined. There can be no complaint, therefore, if British be substituted for French refined, even though the perfidious British refiner should thereby enjoy an increase in his business. But it would seem as if Sir Thomas Farrer and his friends thought that alone a sufficient reason for condemning the abolition of bounties. And it must be recollected that it is for the purpose of abolishing bounties, not of excluding competitors, that refiners and producers have urged the acceptance of the remedy so persistently insisted on by the French Government as the only security to the contracting Powers against bounty-fed competition. The sugar trade of this country and our colonies have asserted, till they are tired of repeating it, that they do not desire or expect to stop foreign competition by the abolition of bounties, but only to stop the artificial profit against which no natural industry can eventually survive.

The United States, Sir Thomas Farrer says, are to keep their immense markets open to the French sugar which he erroneously assumes that we are about to reject.

Here he has fallen unconsciously and through ignorance of his subject into an error which is fatal to his argument. The French exports consist of sugar which, under the laws of the United States, would be struck with a prohibitive duty, and therefore could not find an outlet in the United States. He speaks of other nations, whose "immense markets" are open to the sugar we reject. What nations? Where are these immense markets? But it does not matter, for Sir Thomas Farrer admits in another place, as has been already pointed out, that the whole thing, however big it may be, only amounts to an exchange of one sugar for another, in which no one will suffer, while British and Colonial interests will benefit, and the consumer will secure the free and open competition of those sugar producers throughout the world who have hitherto been repressed by bounty-fed competition. Natural production will expand to its natural limits, and this country, like all the rest of the world, will reap the benefit of the increased supply. Sir Thomas Farrer is, in fact, lamenting over an imaginary loss of the protected article, and his lamentations are raised in the name of Free Trade.

There has been lately more than one practical illustration of the fallacy of Sir Thomas Farrer's view on this question. The United States gave a bounty on refined sugar a few years ago; the result being that very large quantities, more than 100,000 tons, came to this country. When the bounty stopped the importation stopped. On Sir Thomas Farrer's theory, a very large quantity of sugar was suddenly shut out of our markets, which ought to have resulted, if his view be correct, in a partial sugar famine, great rise in price, loss of work to those who make goods to pay for our sugar imports, great injury to the jam trade, and so on. In point of fact, however, the effect was *nil;* the reason being that the void was immediately filled up from elsewhere. The same quantity of sugar was produced, and therefore the same quantity was imported as before.

It is quite useless for Sir Thomas Farrer to suggest that the Sugar Convention is reviving Custom House difficulties, when the same thing has just been done, on a much more serious scale, by imposing on our Customs Authorities the duty of not only prohibiting the importation of goods falsely marked, but also of detecting the false marks. In both cases the remedy will speedily bring about the desired cure; but in the case of bounties the cure will come without the application of the remedy. Prevention, in this case, will prove to be better than cure.

The letters in *The Times*, in reply to Sir Thomas Farrer, proved that the abolition of bounties would not increase the price of sugar or decrease the supply. If those proofs were unsound Sir Thomas Farrer had plenty of opportunity, in his subsequent letters which were published in *The Times*, to point out in what way his opponents had failed to prove their case. He made no attempt to do so; he never alluded to the arguments. He now publishes a book, where his opponents naturally expected to find their arguments carefully examined, but where not one single word is said in reference to them. And yet in every chapter, and here again at page 53, Sir Thomas Farrer does not hesitate again to repeat what has been again and again refuted, disposed of, and absolutely pulverised. He says that "the effect of the treaty, if it has any effect, must be to make sugar indefinitely dearer and scarcer than it is." He evidently appreciates the value of iteration. He believes, and perhaps wisely, that he has only to repeat a misstatement often enough, and it will stick in the minds of his readers, while the refutation goes by unheeded or forgotten.

He accuses "the Foreign Office" of having "a leaning
towards Protection." Here he attacks a department, not
the Government ; and this gives us a further insight into the
reasons which have impelled Sir Thomas Farrer to dash
so valiantly into this crusade in favour of protecting the
foreigner on British markets. The Board of Trade, he
complains, were not consulted. Now he tells us that the
Foreign Office has a leaning towards Protection. The inference is obvious. The two departments have evidently
been at loggerheads, and Sir Thomas Farrer has got the
worst of it. The Foreign Office was for Free Trade, the
Board of Trade was for protection to the foreigner on
British markets. The Foreign Office has had its way so
far, but Sir Thomas Farrer and his friends are going to
upset it if they can, and hence his book.

The red herring which is now to be dragged across the
true scent is the endeavour to prove that there is nothing
the matter with the sugar trade. It had a great success a
few years ago, owing to foolish statements of ignorant
people, and the party for which Sir Thomas Farrer acts
no doubt hopes to maintain the false scent and to continue
to divert the public mind from the real and vital question.
It is quite possible that they may succeed ; such red
herrings very often carry away the whole country and
sometimes defeat ministries.

CHAPTER IX.

REPLY TO THE THIRD REJECTED LETTER.

THIS is the red herring chapter. It has nothing to do with the question whether foreign bounties are good things or bad things, whether they should be abolished or encouraged. Sir Thomas Farrer begins, however, by telling us that Mr. Gladstone "determined, notwithstanding the report of Mr. Ritchie's Committee, to maintain a Conservative policy with respect to the sugar bounties." Did he determine to maintain the abuse, the intolerable infringement of the first principles of Free Trade, brought about by bounties protecting foreign producers on British markets? Was this his Conservative policy? We Liberals accuse Conservatives of defending abuses, but certainly they never in these latter days defended a greater abuse than this. Mr. Gladstone's Conservatism must have arisen from the fact that Mr. Ritchie, his political opponent, had shown himself a remarkably able champion of Free Trade principles. Thus one anomaly brought about another, while the sugar trade had to grin and bear it. The Government could not contradict the conclusive and careful report of the Select Committee, so they started, with Sir Thomas Farrer's able assistance, their useful red herring. They could not deny, what the Committee told them in very plain language, that bounties were contrary to Free Trade, and that their abolition, even with the necessary security of a penal clause, was absolutely essential to the restoration of Free Trade. So they seized the opportunity afforded them by foolish exaggerations of ignorant persons, and proceeded to solemnly demonstrate

that neither sugar refining nor sugar planting was yet dead.
If those industries had been dead they would have dragged
their herring in the opposite direction, and pleaded that
it was of no use to come to the rescue of a defunct industry.

Sir Thomas Farrer makes the most of what he calls
" Mr. Chamberlain's Memorandum ; " but we must recollect that Mr. Chamberlain, being new to the work, naturally
took his inspiration from Sir Thomas Farrer, the departmental head of his office. No one doubts for a moment
that the memorandum was written, not by Mr. Chamberlain, but by Sir Thomas Farrer, and that when Sir
Thomas Farrer quotes Mr. Chamberlain he is only quoting
himself. He does not tell his readers that every point in
this memorandum was carefully, and in official form,
answered and refuted, and that the next official document
which appeared from the Board of Trade calmly repeated
the same assertions, without showing any signs of having
received a refutation of them. He withholds this information, but loudly complains that " the negotiators of the
present Convention " have made no attempt to answer the
arguments. Why should they, when a conclusive answer
is found in the Blue Book ? It is for the other side to
complain that the Board of Trade, when convicted of being
in the wrong, took no notice of the reply, but dared to
repeat what it was unable to defend.

But here comes the root of the whole matter, the cause
of all these ten chapters and six appendices. Sir Thomas
Farrer complains bitterly that " on former occasions the
Board of Trade, as the department which represents the
commercial interests of the country [how well it has represented them !] has always been consulted, and its advice,
if not followed, has been listened to with respect." Though
this is only interesting as indicating the true springs of
the present onslaught, and is quite immaterial to the

great question at issue, it must, in passing, be exposed as
entirely untrue and misleading. The Board of Trade has
not been " always consulted." On the contrary, the
Board of Trade had nothing to do with the subject until
quite recently. The history of the change is interesting.
The negotiations about sugar bounties have been going on
for some twenty-five years, and, being international, have
naturally been conducted solely by the Foreign Office, and
its excellent commercial department ; assisted occasionally by able officials from the Customs. Things were well
managed, and a good common-sense view of the necessities
of the case was taken. But a certain Government, when it
came into power, was moved by various considerations connected with the action of its rivals in this matter, to take
the unusual step of removing the conduct of international
negotiations from the Foreign Office to the Board of Trade.
Sir Thomas Farrer then became master of the situation,
and ruled the roost. Of course nothing more was done ;
and this unfortunately happened just at the critical moment
when bounties were having their inevitable effect of enormously stimulating bounty-fed production and grievously
depressing the natural industry. In two or three years
from that date there was such a glut of bounty-fed sugar
that every producer outside the magic ring saw ruin staring
him in the face. And yet we are told to read all the
memorandums that flowed so freely from the Board of
Trade in 1881, when we know that three years later, owing
to the culpable suspension of the negotiations at the instance of the Board of Trade, one of the biggest crises that
ever came upon an industry had arrived, and had most
undoubtedly been caused by the abnormal and sudden
expansion of the beetroot industry arising from the greatly
increased bounty. These facts are notorious to everyone in
the trade. If the crisis of 1884 had not been partially remedied

by a spontaneous reduction in the production of beetroot, coupled with unfavourable weather for the crop, we should have seen a revolution in sugar production which would have involved ruin to many innocent people, and have thrown the trade entirely into the hands of a monopoly. No one can dispute this. Are we to content ourselves with reading memorandums of the Board of Trade, which defend Protection on Free Trade principles, and to remain, in the meantime, periodically subject to this disturbance of our trade? So long as bounties continue to interfere with the arrangements of nature these disturbances will undoubtedly recur, and every time with greater force. Is it any comfort to be told that we are still employing so many men; that the colonies are producing so much sugar? It is greatly to the credit of those who have survived the shock; adversity is, no doubt, good for us all. Even Sir Thomas Farrer might be disposed to take a different view of men and things if he were to taste the wholesome medicine. But surely these figures, these red herrings, are no argument in favour of maintaining and encouraging a system of protection which operates, not in the protected country, but in our own market, and which the other day brought us all, colonial producers and British refiners, within very measurable distance of shutting up shop. And this happened only three years after the Board of Trade undertook to manage the sugar question by issuing erroneous disquisitions on a spurious Free Trade and an imaginary Protection.

Sir Thomas Farrer goes on to ask, " Has the Board of Trade been consulted, and has its advice been suppressed? Or has the Foreign Office been afraid of it, and purposely excluded it from the consultation?" This would be all very amusing if it were not shocking. A great British and Colonial industry is brought within sight of ruin because, for party purposes, a matter is removed from the department properly concerned with its management, and which has dealt with it for nearly twenty years, and transferred to a department which, though it professes to "represent the commercial interests of the country," has for years obstructed those interests in every possible way. Every Government which has been in power since 1862 has not only been in favour of, but has actively undertaken the abolition of the sugar bounties, and yet, at a most critical moment in the progress both of the bounties and of the negotiations for their suppression, for some mysterious reason the whole management is handed over to an official notoriously hostile to the policy which had been followed for twenty years. It is not for him to ask why he was not consulted, but for the trade to demand an explanation of the conduct of the Government, which, without any apparent reason, deliberately handed over their just claims to consideration to the tender mercies of a bitter opponent. The justice of their claims to consideration was being profusely declared on post-cards at the very moment when they were being handed over to the office so well known for its ability "how not to do it."

We are told that "the action of the Government," in allowing the Foreign Office to manage its own affairs, "constitutes a radical change in departmental policy." On the contrary, the taking away from the Foreign Office of a matter purely of international negotiation, and, moreover, of a continuous negotiation which had been going on, under the management of the Foreign Office, for a long series of years, which was still going on, and was on the point of succeeding, is undoubtedly a very radical change in departmental policy. But when to that is added the fact that this long negotiation, so nearly brought to a successful issue, is suddenly handed over to the tender mercies of an official notoriously hostile to its policy, there can be only one inference. The trade can never be too grateful to Mr. Ritchie for the spendid way in which he conducted the inquiry before the Select Committee, which at once stamped him as a man of first-class ability ; but it is to be feared that this exceptionally able conduct of the case by Mr. Ritchie, so sound in every way that his political opponents could not pick a hole in it, stimulated them to take a course which would lead to the subject being shelved, or got rid of by the red herring policy.

If, as Sir Thomas Farrer seems to suspect, the advice of the Board of Trade has been suppressed, he urges that " Parliament has a right to know what the Board of Trade has said." He wants members to be furnished with some more of his " Memorandums." But how could the Board of Trade be suppressed when its Parliamentary secretary was President of the Conference ? Does Sir Thomas Farrer mean to say that Parliament has a right to demand the publication of memorandums drawn up by a sub-ordinate official which his chief has thought proper to disregard ? This would, indeed, be "a radical change in departmental policy." All this is very amusing, but it is difficult for those whose vital interests have been so shame-fully sacrificed while this official comedy has been going on, to treat the matter without some slight disposition to indignation. It was hoped by the Government of that day, that a troublesome and difficult question would be got out of the way, and Sir Thomas Farrer was selected as a most efficient executioner. The culprits have survived and escaped, but the executioner is after them, and is being encouraged with shouts from his former employers.

It is Sir Thomas Farrer who has started this official grievance, and what is said here is strictly in reply to his remarks. He has raised a subject which he had better have left alone, for it is one on which he will most assuredly be worsted.

Now we come to the great indictment against the Government. They have published three Blue Books without an index. Sir Thomas Farrer evidently thinks that things were better managed during the short but happy period when the Board of Trade ruled over the sugar question. But then he forgets that they had washed their hands of international negotiations. They had a soul above such common work as that. Their labours were confined to the periodical issue of "Memorandums"— essays on the promotion of protection to foreigners. Their indexes may have been far superior to those prepared under the auspices of the Foreign Office, but they neglected to indicate to the reader that every assertion of the Board of Trade was answered in the pages of the Blue Book.

The Government have negotiated in the dark, Sir Thomas Farrer says. If so, the darkness must have fallen over the subject during the Farrer memorandum period. An examination of the library of Blue Books will show that previous to that time every conceivable information was in the hands of the Government, without which it would have been impossible to carry on the complicated negotiations which were on the point of success when the Board of Trade intervened, darkness fell, and all was still.

Next he complains that no one has been consulted but sugar planters and sugar refiners. Well, even if this were the case, which it is not, there would be nothing surprising in applying for difficult and technical information about a particular trade to the persons occupied in conducting that trade. But, according to Sir Thomas Farrer, the Board of Trade is the depository of all knowledge, and its only

infallible source. He forgets that an exhaustive inquiry
was held for two years, by a Committee of the House of
Commons, into every fact connected with this complicated
question.   There were plenty of members on that Committee bitterly hostile to the negotiations for the abolition
of bounties, and consequently every corner was ransacked
for evidence to upset the inquiry. Sir Thomas Farrer
cannot, therefore, complain that he and his friends did not
have the amplest opportunity for throwing light upon the
subject.   The evidence produced by them does not do
them much credit.   Anyone who cares to read the minutes
cannot fail to see that the Board of Trade and their allies
made a very sorry show.   One gentleman who presented
himself, especially to give information with regard to the
foreign statistics, absolutely did not know the English
equivalent for the Austrian weights.   Theories were propounded by would-be experts in political economy, which
absolutely broke down under Mr. Ritchie's searching
cross-examination.   Everyone was consulted, and it was
quite clear, even in the minority report, that Sir Thomas
Farrer's friends had failed to make out a case.   So much
for the accusation that the Government have consulted no
one.

Sir Thomas Farrer declares I am wrong in saying that
bounties have stimulated production.*   I think the most
uninstructed with regard to the sugar question would at
once admit, as a broad indisputable fact, that producers
who receive a bounty are artificially stimulated to produce
more than they would under natural conditions.   They
have a special extra profit all to themselves, and the natural

* When I get further on in his book I find that he refutes himself
and confirms my statement ; for, at pages 107, 108, he describes the
ruin of Austrian manufacturers, owing to "the unnatural stimulus"
of bounties having caused "a glut."

greediness of human nature inevitably leads them to make
as much of it as they can. Look at the figures to which
Sir Thomas Farrer is so fond of appealing, but which he
likes to arrange in his own way. In 1863-4 the European
beetroot crop was 349,000 tons; in 1886-7 it was 2,730,206
tons. Can any one say that, the fact of heavy bounties on
beetroot sugar being now fully admitted, these bounties
have had nothing to do with this enormous increase in
production? Certainly the people most capable of judging,
the beetroot producers themselves, distinctly declare that
their industry has been stimulated by bounties.

Then Sir Thomas Farrer says that I contradict this
assertion by maintaining that the abolition of bounties,
"coupled with the exclusion of some of our ways of supply," would not lessen supply nor raise price. I am not
responsible for the English, but I certainly maintain the
fact, which is in no way incompatible with the other fact.
The beetroot industry is now firmly established as one of
the most valuable on the continent of Europe. It will
continue now to flourish, bounties or no bounties. But if
bounties go on, it will continue to do what it did in 1884,
over-produce, and injure itself as well as others. We don't
want over-production; we dont want glutted markets.
They are bad for all, producers and consumers, merchants
and dealers, for they are invariably followed by a reaction
which goes as much too far in the other direction, and, in
the case of an artificially stimulated glut like this, they are
followed by the much more serious result of injury and ob-
struction to the natural sources of production. The other
point, the old one so often answered, which now figures in
curious language as "the exclusion of some of our ways of
supply," is thus well disposed of by Mr. Shepheard in his
able paper which is printed in the Appendix. "We now
come to the last proposition, 'that prohibition of imports of

bounty-aided sugar is a restriction on imports of sugar.' This we deny, and, on the contrary, say that it is simply the prohibition of bounties, not of sugar. It is the substitution of sugar without bounty for sugar with bounty. If sugar wrapped in blue paper was excluded, whilst that wrapped in white paper was admitted, there would be no restriction on imports of sugar, but simply of the blue paper wrappers. We secure the Free Trade wrapper for our sugar by excluding the Protectionist wrapper of a bounty."

It is only necessary to add to this that, as there is plenty of Free Trade sugar, and as the quantity of it will be greatly increased by the conversion of protected sugar into Free Trade sugar under the terms of the Convention, there will be no reduction of supply. The price will, in any case, be the price ruling throughout the world. It is marvellous that any intelligent person should not see all this, or should imagine that any one possessed of ordinary common sense could possibly be deceived by such a transparent fallacy as this which Sir Thomas Farrer is so fond of repeating, and which he makes the sheet-anchor on which his whole position depends.

The next criticism is on the figures quoted by Baron de Worms, giving the amount of the bounties in various countries. The figures are the result of a careful examination of the evidence furnished by the official statistics and financial statements of the several countries, and have been arrived at by one of the most eminent sugar statisticians in Germany. In this case, therefore, it is not true to accuse our Government of having consulted no one but sugar planters and sugar refiners. Of course, however, Sir Thomas Farrer wants to make out that they are all wrong. He does not tell us where they are wrong, or what the right ones are. He has, by-the-bye, misprinted the figures, which is a bad habit when figures are regarded as the strong point. As to the flat contradiction of Baron de Worms' assertion, that the object of these bounties is to develop the industry, it is only necessary to say that however the bounties originated, which is now a long time ago, they have undoubtedly been allowed to continue after their existence had been discovered, for the purpose indicated by Baron de Worms. This is fully proved in every number of every foreign journal connected with the beetroot industry for the last twenty years, and in every debate which has taken place in foreign Parliaments on the question. France deliberately established an enormous new bounty in 1884, because her industry could not otherwise compete against the other European bounties. All this is on record in the columns of the *Journal Officiel*. But what grounds has Sir Thomas Farrer for assuming that the other bounties were not intentional? Let him examine the evidence taken before the Superior Council of Commerce in Paris in 1872, and he will find it distinctly stated by one of the witnesses that the bounty to the refiners, which had been going on for long, was clearly foreseen and intended by those who originated the system under which it was obtained. Why should not the same have been the case with regard to duty on the roots in Germany, duty on the density of the juice in Holland and Belgium, and duty on the capacity of the apparatus in Austria? We know from long experience how carefully foreign Governments frame their fiscal legislation with a view to encouraging industry, and it must have been evident to the originators of these various laws that they would inevitably give a bounty. The matter has little bearing on the question, but I have undertaken to reply fully to Sir Thomas Farrer's letters, and I find that even on collateral points and in parenthetical remarks he is generally wrong. He wants to know why the French bounty is calculated on the quantity produced. The reason

F

is that the fact of the bounty being obtainable on export
enables the producer to obtain it on his whole production.
He exports his surplus and makes the home consumer pay
him the full duty-paid value on the remainder, he having
paid less than the full duty. The same applies to Germany,
and therefore, to have been strictly parallel, the calculation
should have been made in the same way. But it is quite
immaterial. The important point is to know how much
artificial profit is being made. Sir Thomas Farrer says he
is unable to prove or check these figures. He could if he
tried, but it would involve a considerable knowledge of the
European Sugar Trade, the fiscal systems and revenue
returns of the various countries, and a multitude of the
other details, in all of which the Board of Trade have displayed absolute ignorance. It is a curious fact, not
generally known, that even the monthly statistics called
"the Board of Trade returns" are in great part returns the
details of which are absolutely unknown to the Board of
Trade. The statistical office of Her Majesty's Customs
really compiles many of these figures—knows all about them,
where they come from, what they mean. The Board of
Trade knows none of these things. It merely receives the
figures, puts its name on them, and gets the whole of the
credit. The Custom House does all the work and gets
none of the glory. I am glad to have this opportunity of
doing justice to a most able and industrious department,
which has too long been overshadowed by those who get
the lion's share, and, like the lion, get others to do the work
for them.

Because, as he confesses, he is ignorant of the origin of
these figures, and knows not how they are estimated, Sir
Thomas Farrer assumes that no one else can know. I
recommend him a course of reading for his leisure hours:
the *Deutsche Zuckerindustrie*, the *Journal des Fabricants de*

Sucre, and the *Sucrerie Indigène*, are published weekly; the *Sucrerie Belge* fortnightly. He will find in these papers that facts and figures are not dealt with abroad in a slipshod way, nor by those who are not fully up in their subject. It would give him a new insight into statistical methods and the examination of results. He will then find that others have succeeded where he has either failed or, as is more probable, has never made an effort.

Whatever may be his ignorance of detail, however, one thing, he says, is certain, that the abolition of these bounties of nine millions a year "must inevitably have the consequence of diminishing the supply, and raising the price to the consumers of this country." A foot-note says, "See further on this point, Letter IV." It should have been, "See further on this point, *passim*."

The reply has been given so often that I will not repeat it, because the context furnishes me with a new one. Germany gave the other day a bounty of £3,238,484—her own figures. That bounty has been greatly reduced, and the German Government has prepared a Bill for its total abolition. Does any one suppose that the German Government would do that if it thought that it would reduce a production which has done more for the welfare of the country during many years than any other industry? It has been the salvation of German agriculture; it has given employment to untold numbers, both in the factories and the fields—employment also at the very time of year when work is scarcest; it has given a vast stimulus to the makers of machinery, who have for years done, and are still doing, an enormous trade in the manufacture of the very considerable plant necessary for sugar manufacture; it has greatly increased the head of cattle in all the countries where it is carried on; it has been one of the largest customers to the artificial manure makers and

importers. The railways, canals, and navigable rivers, are
loaded, sometimes with roots for the factory, sometimes
with sugar for export or home consumption, sometimes
with pulp for cattle, often with machinery for new factories,
or new machinery for old ones. Look, too, at the vast
consumption of coal necessary to evaporate the juice
expressed from nine million tons of roots, and the employment involved in the production and carriage of such a
quantity of fuel. Is the German Government deliberately
aiming a blow at such an industry as this? No; the
German Government, like the German industry and its
literary organs, knows a good deal more about sugar and
the sugar question than Sir Thomas Farrer and the Board
of Trade ever dreamt of. The statistician of that department could not even tell the Select Committee what
English weight was equivalent to a metrical centner, so it
is clear that the department had not gone deeply into the
facts and figures connected with this vast industry. It has
no means of judging, therefore, what will happen to the
industry when it loses the remainder of its bounty. That
the German Government does know is quite clear from the
action it has taken, and it is evident that its views on a
matter with which it is perfectly conversant are diametri-
cally opposed to those of Sir Thomas Farrer.

We come now to British figures. Baron De Worms
quoted the percentages of cane and beet in our imports
since 1852. Sir Thomas Farrer puts a foot-note : " I have
not checked them, and cannot find them in the published
returns." He evidently regards any figures which do not
bear the Board of Trade mark as inevitably stamped with
the brand of inaccuracy. He could have checked them in
five minutes, but he did not do so. He prefers to remain
ignorant, and throw a vague doubt upon them in a foot-
note.

He goes on to say that these figures have nothing to do with the matter, because, in point of fact, the production of cane sugar has not diminished. Yes, but how much has beetroot increased in the last twenty to twenty-five years? It has increased eightfold. The figures quoted by Baron de Worms have, therefore, a great deal to do with the subject.

Then come some West Indian figures, which Sir Thomas Farrer condemns because they are hypothetical. That all depends on the value of the hypothesis, and that he declines to examine. He takes the opportunity, however, of branding the West Indian proprietors as "an interest seeking Protection." The word with the capital P is always brought in wherever possible, and especially when a serious discussion has to be avoided. Bounties are Protection to the foreign producer on British markets. Sir Thomas Farrer considers that those who desire this protection removed are "seeking Protection." He never tells us why or how, but he lays it down as one of the dogmas which, as they are published by the Cobden Club, must be accepted as infallible.

So far Sir Thomas Farrer seems to have broken down about the facts. But he, on the contrary, seems quite pleased, for he opens his next subject by saying, "This disposes, so far as I can find out, of all the facts, or supposed facts, relating to the sugar trade which are produced by the Government in support of the change which they propose." As I have shown, his method of "disposing of" the figures is by saying that he never heard of them, cannot check them, is unable to prove them, cannot find them in the published returns, and so on. His remarks and criticisms I have shown to be, in every case, erroneous. The figures could have been checked, and the origin and accuracy of them ascertained if he had desired.

But he only desired to discredit them, and therefore it was better not to ascertain their accuracy. But what does Sir Thomas Farrer mean by saying that these are the only facts and figures in support of the change which the Government proposes? There is a great library of Blue Books on the subject, extending back to the time when the international negotiations began, in 1862. Those negotiations have gone on ever since, except during Sir Thomas Farrer's short and useful reign. During the whole of that time successive Governments were accumulating information on the subject, all of which is on record in the Blue Books. Then came the Select Committee, the minutes of its evidence, and its reports. And yet the Government is now accused by Sir Thomas Farrer of taking action on insufficient information. Was there ever a more outrageous assertion? The Government are, in fact, merely continuing negotiations which were nearly successful ten years ago, but which were suddenly upset by the transfer of the conduct of the question from the Foreign Office to the Board of Trade, a transfer which thoroughly answered its purpose of getting rid of a troublesome business, and allowed the sugar industries no alternative but to take the advice of the Board of Trade and combat bounties by a reduction of wages.

In spite of all this mass of information, accumulated during twenty-five years of constant negotiation, and an inquiry by a Parliamentary Committee, which extended through two sessions, Sir Thomas Farrer says that "Government ought to be called on to give a new exhaustive report upon the present condition of the trade." He wants to show, what every one knows, that the trade is not dead. If it were there would be no outcry against sugar bounties. Dead people give no trouble.

He begins his "attempt to state some facts" by comparing production in 1872 with that in 1886. He has chosen years favourable to the complexion he wishes to put on the comparison. But it does not matter, because the fact of our having survived is no argument against remedying such an evil as bounty-fed competition. He cannot show from these figures what struggles sugar production has gone through in competing against an artificial profit, nor what struggles it will have to face in the future if this artificial profit is to continue the main factor in the trade. It is, therefore, hardly worth pointing out errors in his statement, or in the inference he draws from it. I think he will find, if he examines the sources from which these figures are drawn, that the list of British cane sugar which supplies his figures for 1872 omits some countries which are included in the list for 1886. In drawing his inference he forgets that large sugar industries, such as those in Australia and the Sandwich Islands, have sprung up since 1872, the first being for many years independent of bounty influences, and the second being stimulated by the fact that its sugar was sold in the United States at the duty-paid price without having paid any duty. However, these are only minor points. It does British colonial enterprise great credit to have held its own so many years against such long odds. But the question for the Government to consider is the future. It is only during these last few years, since 1883, that the great glut has arrived. If the bounties continue the crisis will not be removed, but aggravated. The German Government see this perfectly well, and so do many other people on the Continent. The British Government have, therefore, done valuable service, even to the beetroot trade itself, by helping to bring about this international agreement.

Sir Thomas Farrer speaks of Java having increased its

production " in spite of the abolition of a bounty on export
which formerly existed." Does he not mean the regulations by which the Java planters were compelled to send
their sugar to Holland—regulations which they were
thankful to get rid of, and the abolition of which did much
to give an impulse to their industry ?

Of course, there are other causes operating on the sugar
trade, just as there are on everything else in the world.
No one is so foolish as to maintain that the only influence
which has been exercised on the sugar trade of the world
has been that of bounties. Demerara has increased its
production because it invented a new kind of sugar which
has been very popular, and has always commanded a high
price. But even Demerara was in a bad way in 1884, when
the big beetroot crop drove prices down to ruination point.
It does not follow, because production does not immediately
fall off, that therefore there is no suffering or difficulty or
danger. Producers keep going long after those troubles
have shown above the horizon. They even increase production in bad times, so as to reduce working expenses.
Sir Thomas Farrer does not tell us who drew the inference
from Baron de Worms' figures, that beetroot is killing cane
sugar. There is no need to draw any inference at all
from the figures. They simply announce the fact that
beetroot has to a great extent supplanted cane in our
markets. In refined sugar alone we now have 350,000
tons of foreign refined beetroot where we formerly had
none. And yet Sir Thomas Farrer thinks that he has
disposed of Baron de Worms' figures because he shows that
beet sugar has not killed cane sugar.

Cane sugar, he points out, has gone elsewhere. Certainly it has, but when the bounty-fed glut comes, such as
that of 1884, it does not escape the effect of it. If sugar
becomes a drug in the market in Europe, so it does in

America. Even Australia now feels it, and cries out loudly for the abolition of bounties. He says his figures prove that cane sugar can hold its own. All that they prove is that it has held its own, but they do not demonstrate, which is the whole point of the question, whether it can stand another year like 1884. Such a year will speedily come again if bounties continue.

The next paragraph begins : " Beet sugar, then, has not displaced cane sugar in the world generally." This is a curious conclusion to come to when, as I have shown, it appears that the beetroot production has, during the last twenty-five years, been multiplied by eight, and that it now constitutes half—more than half—the total visible production of the world ; whereas then it was but a drop in the ocean. I am not very old, and yet I recollect the first sample of beetroot sugar ever seen in Mincing Lane. Some slight change must have taken place since then in the relative proportions of beet and cane, although Sir Thomas Farrer does lay it down as one of his dogmas to be swallowed by all believers, that " beet sugar has not displaced cane sugar in the world generally." Why, even the United States have imported 25,000 tons of beetroot sugar since the 1st of January. Sir Thomas Farrer must give us some better statistics than those contained in Mr. Picton's return before he will make us believe this new and startling information.

We are then told that "beet growers are at this moment much alarmed at the future possibilities of cane sugar, when the same science shall have been applied to its manufacture as is now applied to beet." How carefully he suppresses the real reason for their alarm, which he will find fully stated in the foreign journals which I have already recommended to his notice. He will there find it fully set out, that the abolition of bounties will enable capitalists to embark in undertakings in cane sugar countries which they would never think of risking till bounties were out of the way. This will lead to improved culture, improved manufacture, increased production, and reduced cost. This is exactly what we ask for in the name of Free Trade, and which Sir Thomas Farrer opposes for reasons best known to himself, but which he has utterly failed to expound successfully in this or any other book.

Undoubtedly there are many causes for the production of beetroot sugar. No one ever imagined that it was produced because there happened to be bounties. I myself took a leading part, in the year 1871, in advocating the introduction of the crop into this country. Under Free Trade conditions it is a crop and an industry which would be the salvation of the British farmer, and a godsend to the rural population, more especially in the winter months. It furnishes an excellent food for cattle. The high cultivation necessary for its growth greatly improves the land, and thus increases the yield of wheat. All these facts, in addition to Sir Thomas Farrer's eulogium, prove that we are losing a most valuable addition to our agricultural enterprises. But would anyone in his senses embark in this most desirable pursuit, so long as his Continental competitors received a bounty? It turns out, therefore, that Sir Thomas Farrer's beetroot eulogy is one more argument, and one of the strongest, for the abolition of bounties. I am grateful to him for having brought up a matter which has always appeared to me of the very highest importance to this country, and which is much more urgently called for in the present condition of our agricultural industry than it was when I took it up in 1871.

This leads Sir Thomas Farrer on to another point, which also turns out on examination to tell strongly

against him, and to cry out loud for the abolition of
bounties. He is still seeking for reasons to account for the
production of beetroot sugar, and for its beating cane
sugar. He declines even to recognise the fact that beet
beats cane because it receives a bounty, though he now
fully admits the existence of the bounty. He therefore
argues that cane is beaten because " whilst capital, science,
and industry have done their utmost for beet, cane has not
generally had the same advantages." This is the main
ground on which our colonial producers demand the
abolition of bounties. The very reason which has enabled
the beetroot industry to apply with lavish hand every improvement of modern science, has stood in the way of
improvement in cane sugar. The beetroot growers and
manufacturers, by means of the extra profit obtained by
the bounty, have had ample capital to embark in costly
machinery, expensive experiments, and generous farming.
The colonial producer, on the other hand, has had hanging
over his head the deterring influence of a bounty-fed competition. He hesitates to embark capital in improvements
and extended cultivation, so long as bounties continue.
He knows that they must bring back a recurrence of such
disastrous years as 1884. He wants Free Trade, but Sir
Thomas Farrer won't let him have it.

We now jump to a different subject. Sir Thomas
Farrer tells us that loaf sugar has almost disappeared, and
has been replaced by lump sugar. We who manufacture
that article always thought that the two words were
synonymous. However, it is of no consequence, as the
matter appears to have no connection with the abolition of
bounties. But when Sir Thomas Farrer says that loaf
sugar has almost disappeared, he wanders considerably
from the path of accuracy, for it certainly appears to us
who make it that the consumption goes on increasing

rapidly. In correction of another statement, it may be
mentioned as an historical fact, that in 1875 the French
bounty on loaf sugar, which then reached its zenith and
immediately declined rapidly, had succeeded in shutting up
every loaf-sugar refinery in this country, only one of which
survived the shock. Of course new ones have sprung up
since the bounty was reduced, for the competition has now
been transferred to crystallised and granulated sugars, as
I foretold in my evidence before the Select Committee in
1879.

Sir Thomas Farrer explains that crystallised and
granulated sugars are made at the place of original
production, and he desires his readers to infer that it is
for this reason, and not because of the bounty, that they
interfere with the British refiner. But it is the extra profit
of the bounty which hurts us, not the production of the
sugar. We have for years asserted that it is not the
importation of foreign sugar that we object to, but the
bounty, which destroys free and open competition.

The manufacture of sugar is undoubtedly improving
all over the world, as Sir Thomas Farrer explains, but
what has this to do with the abolition of bounties?
He says it shows how dangerous it would be to keep
up an industry by artificial means. We, on the other
hand, say that it is dangerous to all parties, especially
the consumer, to keep down an industry by artificial means.
We ask, therefore, that the artificial disturbance caused
by the bounty shall be removed, and Sir Thomas Farrer
condemns this removal on the ground that it would
be keeping up an industry by artificial means. He
desires to mystify his readers, and he is very likely to
succeed with a certain class, but not with those who take
the trouble to think.

Sir Thomas Farrer declines to give recent Board of

Trade returns, which would have shown the enormous increase in the importation of foreign refined sugar, because, he says, he is not quite sure that raw and refined sugar have the same meaning now which they had in 1880. If he likes to inquire at the Custom House, where the returns are made up, he will find that there is just as distinct a line of demarcation between the two kinds, and one identically the same now as it was then. The 350,000 tons of refined sugar which we now annually import from abroad are, in fact, more absolutely refined than the few thousand tons which we imported in the old days before bounties, and which were taken for transhipment to other ports.

Now we come to the figures by which Sir Thomas Farrer proves that sugar refining, like cane sugar production, is not dead. I might quote him by saying that, with regard to these figures, " it would be satisfactory to know where they come from, how they are estimated ; " but it is not worth while, though I happen to know that, in regard to one of the centres of the industry, the figures were procured from a person who had no means of knowing the facts but simply guessed at them, and that consequently they are incorrect. But it is absolutely immaterial, because the larger the industry the more important it is to defend it against such a competition, such a subversion of every principle of Free Trade, as is involved in the protection of foreigners on British markets by means of bounties.

We who ought to understand our own business are told, by one who cannot possibly have more than a most superficial knowledge of it, this astounding piece of news, that " if refining is diminishing, it can scarcely be due to bounties, since the refiners receive in the price of the unrefined yellow beet sugar full compensation for the bounties on foreign white sugar." It is, to us who are in the trade, almost impossible to believe that anyone could for a moment conceive an idea so absolutely devoid of all reasonable foundation. Our opponents must indeed be hard up for arguments when they have recourse to such a miserable, or rather such a comic argument as this. We are competing against foreign refiners, whose raw material is this very "unrefined yellow beet sugar" of which Sir Thoms Farrer speaks. If we buy it, we give the same price for it as our foreign competitor does, and we have to pay the carriage on it. We both turn it into refined sugar, on which he gets a bounty and we do not; and yet this "unrefined yellow beet sugar," which we both buy at the same price, but on which we have to pay the carriage, compensates us in some mysterious way, only known to Sir Thomas Farrer and his friends, for the bounty which our foreign competitor enjoys. It is trifling with intelligent readers to advance such arguments as these.

It is remarked in a foot-note to this, though with what object is not apparent, that according to report the sugar trade is now doing much better. Why? Because there was a short beetroot crop, very slightly short, but just enough to give a little temporary relief from the fierce onslaught of foreign competition.

The labour employed by trades subsidiary to sugar refining would, according to Sir Thomas Farrer, be employed in any case, because "other trades of a like nature are equally called into existence by the businesses to which the employment of foreign sugar gives rise." Does Sir Thomas Farrer seriously believe—or is he only throwing dust in our eyes—that foreign refined sugar calls into existence any "businesses" which would not be equally called into existence if the refined sugar were made here?

He is pleased to have demonstrated "that the business

of refining is not dead in England." No one ever said it was. But he admits that " British refineries have suffered loss of profit in recent years ; " though he adds, without a shadow of foundation for the statement, " but not more than their foreign bounty-fed competitors have notoriously suffered." Where are the usual array of figures in proof of this most erroneous statement? It is notorious, on the contrary, that refiners in all European countries, except the United Kingdom, have been making large fortunes out of the bounty.

Now we come to that celebrated red herring, "the jam argument." It has been disposed of many, many times, but here it is again, though none of the replies to it have ever been dealt with or even referred to. Is it the little sixpence per hundredweight, by which the British refiner is undersold, that brings the vast jam trade into existence ? Or is it the low prices for raw sugar, which did not begin till 1884? If the former, the thing is absurd, because such an amount as that only represents the ordinary daily fluctuations of the market, and can have no possible effect on the use of sugar. If the latter be what Sir Thomas Farrer means—there is no other alternative—then all this wonderful expansion in the jam industry must have taken place in the last four years. But if Sir Thomas Farrer examines the yearly consumption of sugar, he will find that the rate of increase has actually been less since 1884 than it was before. If the jam industry expanded before 1884, it did so for other reasons than those put forward by him. The real reason was, of course, the abolition of the sugar duty. But Sir Thomas Farrer wishes it to be believed that bounties have had something to do with it, so that he may marshal his figures and show that the destruction of the refining industry would be the salvation of the jam industry. A letter appeared in the *Times* some time ago from Messrs. Keiller and Son, the well-known jam, marmalade, and confectionery manufacturers, contradicting all this; but even such a contradiction has no effect on Sir Thomas Farrer when he gets hold of a favourite red herring. It has done him great service and made an immense impression on that curious structure called the public mind. He will no doubt go on hammering away at it as long as it draws. He quite ignores also the fact, so frequently proved, that sugar will be just as cheap after bounties are abolished as it is now, probably cheaper, since there will be a great expansion in the production of cane sugar, which, by the way, all good jam makers much prefer to beetroot.

It is curious that Sir Thomas Farrer is obliged to have recourse to a Vienna paper in order to enlighten his readers as to the state of our home trade, and neglects to examine or quote from foreign papers when they deal with matters connected with their own industry, with which they must inevitably be better acquainted than Sir Thomas Farrer.

The use of sugar in brewing and cattle feeding has, in the opinion of Sir Thomas Farrer, an important bearing on the question of bounties. Does he mean that less sugar would be used for these purposes if there were no bounty? If so, the idea is so absurd as to be quite unworthy of discussion. Again I repeat, that sugar will be as cheap, if not cheaper, after the abolition of bounties than it is now. Moreover, brewers must have cane sugar, and so must cattle. The abolition of bounties will therefore be a positive advantage to both those interests. And yet Sir Thomas Farrer laments that these important "facts" are carefully concealed from the Government by the cunning representatives of the sugar trade; "they are not among the promptings of the refiners and West Indian planters, to whom alone Ministers seem to listen." The

real fact being that these "facts" have been thoroughly
exposed long ago, and shown to have no foundation. As
to prompting the Government, I never, during the long
course of my experience in this question, saw a Government so ready to take its own line, so absolutely independent of all species of prompting. This is very natural,
considering the great mass of accumulated information and
evidence which they have before them.

Sir Thomas Farrer next turns his attention to consumption and price, but his figures are not so cleverly
handled as usual. He tries in general terms to make
out that the low prices, which of course he desires his
readers to suppose to arise from bounties, have enormously
increased consumption. The consumption was greatly
increased by the gradual reduction and final abolition of
the duty. But if he desires to deal with the really low
prices brought about by the over-production of beetroot
sugar, which only began in 1884, then, as I said just now,
he will find that the rate of increase in consumption has
not been greater since that date than it was before. As
a matter of fact, curiously enough, the rate of increase has
been rather less.

The cost of sugar to foreign consumers is, he urges,
" at least twice, and often probably much more than twice,
what it is in England." Well, that entirely depends upon
the amount of duty levied upon it. Whatever that amount
may be is the only measure of the increased cost to the
foreign consumer. In fact, Sir Thomas Farrer is merely
singing the praises of the abolition of the duty in this
country; but he wants his readers to believe that all the
benefit arising from that measure is the result of our enjoying bounty-fed sugar. If he does not mean that, what
is he driving at? "It is folly," he says, "to endanger
such results for the purpose of protecting industries so

G

comparatively small and so precarious as sugar refining
and West India planting." The results to which he refers
are, as I have said, purely results of the abolition of the
duty. By "protecting" us, he means abolishing the
bounties.

The abolition of bounties will, as I have shown, undoubtedly give us a better and more uniform supply of
sugar, and will, therefore, intensify instead of endangering,
the advantages we now enjoy from having duty-free
sugar. The abolition of bounties will also relieve the
sugar refiners and West India planters from Sir Thomas
Farrer's imputation of being "small" and "precarious" industries, because they will expand in size and strengthen
in constitution. This, like so many of Sir Thomas
Farrer's contentions, is what people call a specious
argument. I should be disposed to call it by a stronger
name. I cannot imagine that those who advance such
arguments really believe in them. It is still more difficult to appreciate the position of those readers who not
only swallow such arguments but call them "weighty."

But I find, in the next paragraph, that I am quoted in
support of these fallacies. I must first correct the quotation. What I said was that a short beetroot crop had on
more than one occasion actually caused a rise of 50 per
cent. in the value of sugar. This was in proof of the contention that the consumer is becoming more and more
dependent on the beetroot crop. Sir Thomas Farrer
now asks, if this be so, how much more would the
stoppage of the bounty or the exclusion of the bounty-fed
sugar affect price? The answer is obvious. A short crop
reduces the supply of the world, and, therefore, raises
prices. The abolition of bounties will not reduce the
supply of the world, nor will the prohibition of bounty-
fed sugar, and, therefore, prices will not be affected by either

of these contingencies. Again, I ask, is such a fallacy really believed by those who propound it, or is it all make-believe? And yet the chapter ends with the jubilant cry, that these alone are sufficient reasons for rejecting the Convention, and that the case against it has now become overwhelming. Those who are asking for arguments with which to defeat the Government must be thankful for small mercies if these are the best they can get.

CHAPTER X.

REPLY TO THE FOURTH REJECTED LETTER.

A FOOTNOTE at the end of the last chapter catches my eye.
The fact that a slight reduction in the enormous beetroot crop
is now sufficient to raise prices 50 per cent. is caught at by
Sir Thomas Farrer as being a dangerous admission, because
if there were no beetroot we should only have cane sugar
to depend upon. Quite so, and if there were no cane we
should only have beetroot to fall back upon. Let bounties
go on long enough, and we shall soon see what even an
approach to that state of things will bring about. As it
is, we are now so dependent on beetroot that every fluctuation in the crop causes a much more violent fluctuation in
the market. This is an artificial state of things which only
the abolition of bounties will remedy. We want to see a
cane sugar crop big enough to make us quite indifferent
to the changeable weather on the Continent. This is
necessary if the consumer is to get a steady supply of cheap
sugar. But Sir Thomas Farrer is determined that we shall
not have that if he can help. He ends his footnote by
talking about the old times (1779), when we were dependent entirely on West India sugar, and therefore a cyclone
caused a big rise. This is exactly my case. Let us have
Free Trade in sugar, and then market prices will not be
governed by one particular and comparatively small area
of production.*

* Since writing the above a "boom" has occurred in the sugar
market, entirely owing to our dependence on the bounty-stimulated
beetroot crop. A trade circular of March 29th says: "It is now
evident, as was foreseen might be the case, that the holders on the

This new chapter is all about America. Sir Thomas Farrer's point is that if " the cheap French sugar " is prohibited in Europe, because France won't agree to the Convention which she was so active in negotiating—an improbable supposition—this " cheap French sugar " will then go to the United States and displace " inferior cane sugar." France will have a large market and will snap her fingers at everybody. But Sir Thomas Farrer is evidently not aware that France wants to export refined sugar, and those kinds of sugar which are absolutely excluded from the United States by prohibitive duties. Things will, therefore, not be quite so easy for France as Sir Thomas Farrer imagines. This disposes of the principal contention in this chapter.

Please note that sugar refining in the United States employs 150,000 men, as quoted from an official report by Sir Thomas Farrer; and that the United States do not import bounty-fed refined sugar. The number of men estimated by Sir Thomas Farrer to be employed by British refiners is 4,260. The difference in the quantity turned out in the two countries must indeed be large if the American refiners employ 150,000 men against our 4,260. It is more than thirty-five times as many, and this in a country where labour-saving is carried much further than with us. How does Sir Thomas Farrer explain this extraordinary discrepancy between two countries whose consumption is almost identical?

Note again that this official report proceeds with its description of the United States refining industry as follows :—" It is one in which large fortunes have been

Continent have the immediate future of the market much in their hands, owing to the reduction of stocks in Europe and America, as well as to the decrease in some of the leading sources of cane production."

made under a system of drawback rates, which for this reason is not likely to be abandoned. That the drawback rates at present allowed act as a bounty cannot be denied." But at page 64 Sir Thomas Farrer says:—"British refineries have suffered loss of profit in recent years, but not more than their foreign bounty-fed competitors have notoriously suffered." Here we have Her Majesty's Minister at Washington (Commercial, No. 15, 1888; No. 141, page 91) telling us exactly the reverse of what Sir Thomas Farrer tells us. The American refiners are making large fortunes out of a bounty which used to be two shillings per hundredweight, but which is now reduced to less than one, and yet we are told that foreign refiners, many of whom receive much higher bounties than the Americans, are suffering from loss of profit just as severely as the British refiners. Of course we who are in the trade know that this is untrue, but it is satisfactory to drop upon an official document which contradicts it so thoroughly.

Having arrived at the conclusion that the United States are about to play an important part both as producers and refiners, Sir Thomas Farrer proceeds to say that, as regards export bounties, they are in precisely the same position as the bounty-giving countries of Europe. This is an error; there is no export bounty on the sugar produced in the United States, and a very minor one now on the sugar refined from imported sugar. This small remnant of a bounty will undoubtedly be done away with as soon as the United States Government is made to understand that it is a bounty, and that matters will be facilitated by its abolition. The United States Government must be fully alive to the advantage which would accrue to their own sugar-growers by the abolition of bounty-fed competition. This is of still greater importance if Sir Thomas Farrer is right in assuming that sugar production is about to increase

largely in the United States. Producers there do not
desire that the market should be periodically glutted by
an artificially stimulated production. They will, therefore,
do all they can to promote the present effort for the
abolition of bounties. It is not at all likely, therefore,
that the United States will ever come under the penal
clause.

The error is repeated here as to the proposed bounty
to counterbalance the loss of duty to the Louisiana planters.
It is not an export bounty.

Sir Thomas Farrer paints an alarming picture of this
country "quarrelling with her own best friends," and
"depriving herself of the produce—all the contingent
produce—of that great country." The answer, in addition
to that which I have already given, is that the production
of the United States is not more than a tenth part of its
consumption, and that, therefore, it will be a very long
time before it becomes an exporter of its own sugar.
Probably that time will never arrive.

He speaks of the United States making this country a
free gift of sugar. This is nonsense. Sugar is sold at the
market price of the day, whatever may be its origin.
There are never two prices in the same market, nor is
sugar ever given away.

Then comes the great question of the most-favoured-
nation clause. It is curious that Sir Thomas Farrer
should have raised this important point à propos of the
United States; because it happens to be the United States
that have put the very rational construction on this clause
which would not only make it inoperative in the case of
bounties, but might make it positively instrumental in
compelling their abolition.

The whole question turns upon the interpretation to be
put upon the most-favoured-nation clause. The wording

of the clause is usually unconditional, but it seems that
the United States Government have had occasion, in past
times, to import conditions into its interpretations.

Much more recently our own leading statesmen have
done the same. A debate which took place in the House
of Commons in 1878 gave rise to very interesting ex-
pressions of opinion on this point.

The Attorney-General said: "Now, what was the
meaning of the 'favoured-nation clause'? He took it that in
whatever language that clause might be expressed—and
the language of the different treaties was not always the
same—but whatever language might be used, the real
meaning was this—'You, Great Britain, shall treat us in
the same way as you treat the most favoured nation with
whom you have a treaty; that is to say, you shall treat
us as well as you treat them *under the like circumstances.*'"

The Solicitor-General observed "that the 'favoured-
nation clause' assured equality of rights to all the parties
concerned, but the mistake was to say that that involved
identity of treatment."

Mr. Herschell "quite agreed with the honourable and
learned Solicitor-General that equality of right did not
necessarily mean identity of treatment. But he did say
that equality of right did mean identity of treatment *under
similar circumstances.*"

Mr. Gorst said: "What we had promised to do was
not to establish any prohibition of importation or transit
against the produce of any country with which we had
entered into treaties containing the 'most-favoured-nation
clause,' which would not, *under like circumstances,* be applicable to all other countries."

The Chancellor of the Exchequer said that "this
country was bound to treat all foreign nations alike—but
that was, *alike under similar circumstances.*"

This question of the most-favoured-nation treatment will be found fully dealt with by the Select Committee of the House of Commons on Sugar Industries, both in the evidence taken before the Committee and in its Report.

In 1879 Professor Sheldon Amos, with Mr. W. P. B. Shepheard of Lincoln's-Inn, gave an opinion on the subject, in which they came to the conclusion, after careful examination of all the points, "that imports of sugar into this country may, without contravening the favoured-nation clauses of existing commercial treaties, be distinguished as to countries of origin wherein bounties on export are or are not obtainable, and a countervailing duty levied on sugar imported from countries where export bounties are obtainable, whilst sugar from all other countries is admitted duty free." . . . "In conclusion we beg to state that our opinion is based upon the broad principle that equality of fiscal condition, as between either Treaty Power and any third country the most favoured by the other Treaty Power, is the object of favoured-nation clauses, and that the one who destroys such equality cannot appeal to the treaty against the act necessitated to reinstate that equality." *

In a speech delivered at a public meeting at the Mansion House, in 1880, Mr. Arthur Cohen, Q.C., M.P., said :— " Again, there has been raised a cry about the difficulties to be overcome with respect to the ' favoured-nation ' clauses. On this point, however, I venture to say that no lawyer of much eminence will be found to declare that ' favoured-nation ' clauses preclude our right to levy countervailing duties."

The "suggestion" to which Sir Thomas Farrer refers, with regard to bounties being a breach of the most-favoured-nation clause, has been marvellously distorted in his version of it. A country which has a most-favoured-nation clause treaty with us might very reasonably complain that the treatment of the most favoured nation was not accorded to it, if sugar receiving a bounty was admitted on the same terms as sugar receiving no bounty. The complaint is not against the bounty-giving country, for, as Sir Thomas Farrer puts it, inflicting an injury on England. That is nonsense, and has nothing to do with the point. The complaint is that England admits sugar with a bounty on the same terms as sugar without a bounty, and consequently the sugar-exporting country which gives no bounty loses the equality of treatment stipulated for in the treaty.

The summing-up of the chapter as regards the United States sounds very nice, but need not be dealt with, as I have shown that each portion of the case, from Sir Thomas Farrer's point of view, is without a foundation. It is rather amusing, however, to read of the United States as a country "which may prove to be one of our best sources of supply." The annual consumption of the United States is about 1,500,000 tons, and is going up by leaps and bounds. The production is about 150,000 tons, and is certainly not flourishing. It is very doubtful whether the Louisiana industry can live long, in spite of the large protection it enjoys. But these are the little assertions which deceive the unsuspecting reader, and help to make the whole treatise "weighty."

CHAPTER XI.

REPLY TO NOTES ON BARON DE WORMS' SPEECHES.

THE notes on Baron de Worms' speech are frequently mere
repetitions of what Sir Thomas Farrer says elsewhere. In
such cases I pass them over as already answered For instance, his remarks about the figures which state the amount
annually given in bounty in each country have been dealt
with. He adds a sneer at "Anti-Bounty agitators" who
are accused of having given loose estimates. As I have
frequently, during the last seventeen years, had occasion
to estimate the amount of some of the bounties, and to
give full particulars in support of my calculations, I can
only say, in reply to this accusation, that I have heard
many loose contradictions from Sir Thomas Farrer and his
friends, but have never seen my statements refuted. The
Board of Trade must learn the rudiments of the subject
before they can deal with the difficult technical details
connected with bounties on sugar.

Another variation in this foot-note which requires notice
is the assertion that the bounty operates as an inducement
to export sugar. This is not correct. It operates as an
inducement to over-produce, and to export the surplus
So long as the surplus is exported the producers can obtain
the same amount of bounty on the portion delivered for
home consumption, since they get the full duty-paid value
from the consumer, while they themselves have not paid
the full duty. The rest of the note has already been disposed of. The second note has been answered. On
the third and fourth notes see my remarks. The figures
are not disproved ; they may, therefore, be taken as a

statement of fact. It is difficult to appreciate Sir
Thomas Farrer's angry attack on a statement of fact.
He says, in his marginal abstract of Baron de Worms'
speech: " Beet has supplanted cane in the English
market. Therefore bounties have ruined cane." I have
looked several times at the portion of the speech which
this professes to be an abstract of, but I can find no such
statement. It is very nice for Sir Thomas Farrer's readers
to be able to run their eyes down the margin and thus
be saved the trouble of reading the text of the speech.
It gives them more time thoroughly to enjoy the foot-
notes. But it is not quite fair to print your opponent's
speech with a false marginal abstract.

As to note five, see my replies in another chapter. I
notice in this note the old expression, " cheaper foreign
sugar." All the angry indignation at figures which are
not disproved, expressed by Sir Thomas Farrer in these
foot-notes, should be hushed when he considers the amount
of dust which he is deliberately throwing in the eyes of his
admiring readers.

The conclusion of the note speaks of the Government
" making a great change in our financial policy." What is
this? There is no financial arrangement in the sugar Convention. We have undertaken to apply the principle of
the Trades Marks Act. That is not a financial arrangement. Other countries, it is true, have the option of
levying what they call " surtaxes," because they prefer that
method, it being more in keeping with their commercial
policy.

The sixth note again deals with hypotheses, the value
of which entirely depends on their truth. Sir Thomas
Farrer does not attempt to show that the facts stated are
not facts, nor that the inferences drawn are unsound. He
says he has "been accustomed to a diligent inquiry into

real facts," and therefore his failure to contradict the facts here quoted is the highest possible testimonial to their correctness. This does not prevent him from again abusing the Government.

Note seven is a repetition of a previous one previously dealt with.

Note eight is dealt with elsewhere. As to the "speeches and writings" of "foreign nations," they all go to show that Baron de Worms is right and Sir Thomas Farrer wrong. Everywhere it will be found that the official view abroad is that the abolition or reduction of bounties is a "sacrifice," for which Her Majesty's Government are called upon to be grateful.

The same remarks apply to note nine.

As to note ten, the dispute seems to turn upon the meaning of the word "adhere." Sir Thomas Farrer had asserted that Austria and Belgium had not adhered to the Convention. Baron de Worms says "that is absolutely incorrect." Sir Thomas Farrer, in his foot-note, says, "My statement is absolutely correct," and then begins to tell us about the United States, Sweden, Denmark, and France, all of which information has nothing to do with the correctness or incorrectness of his statement, which referred only to Austria and Belgium. He admits that Austria and Belgium have signed the Convention. Belgium's reservation does not, as he asserts, appear in the Protocol. His foot-note in this case is a decided failure.

The eleventh foot-note gives another opportunity of talking about foreign Ministers making us a present of cheap sugar. If they do so, which I deny, and which I have proved to be untrue, they certainly do not do so without a purpose; and yet Sir Thomas Farrer, in his third foot-note, takes Baron de Worms to task for imputing motives to foreign Governments in giving bounties. Sir

Thomas Farrer has not yet told us why foreign Ministers
give us cheap sugar, though he is very fond of telling us
that they do so. If it be true, surely the British public
will regard such a proceeding with considerable suspicion.
I wonder how Northampton would like foreign Governments to present us with cheap boots and shoes. How
would Leicester like to see its staple products given away
by " foreign Ministers?"

In reply to note twelve, I may remind Sir Thomas
Farrer, in distinct contradiction to one statement, that
the refiners unanimously petitioned the Government to
establish refining in bond, and even offered to pay the
expense. The whole correspondence is in the Blue Books,
and explains fully the former objections.

He blames Baron de Worms for tying our hands so
that we can never revert to protective duties. Curious
language this for the Cobden Club.

The thirteenth note puts one of Sir Thomas Farrer's
fallacies in language which is worth noting. England
" receives the worth in sugar of a subsidy of £9,000,000 a
year." This is Sir Thomas Farrer's view, in his own
words, of the benefit of the bounty to this country. We
know that, in 1881, he made Mr. Chamberlain hint at
some such idea, but now we have it on a larger scale and
in plain language. The real fact, as my readers now know,
is very different. The first operation of a bounty is to
stimulate production. The sugar exported is sold at the
market price, and, therefore, so long as prices are above the
cost of production, the whole of the bounty goes, together with
the natural profit, into the pockets of the producers. When
prices fall, by reason of over-production, below the level of
natural profit, part of the bounty goes to make up for loss
of natural profit. But at the same moment natural producers, having lost their natural profit, are deterred from

proceeding with the competition. If they do proceed, they are giving, out of their own pockets, exactly the same sum as the small fraction of the bounty which has enabled bounty-fed producers to get rid of their over-production without loss. The fraction of the bounty which turns the scale between profit and loss is a very small one; the benefit which importers enjoy is very short-lived, for of course the immediate effect of arrival at cost price is reduction of production and a reaction in the market, which, as recent experience has shown, is violent and injurious. The consumer gets an infinitesimal fraction of the bounty, but only at the moment when cost price is reached; and whatever benefit he gets, he compels natural producers to contribute the same "present" out of their own pockets. This, briefly, is the history of the operation of a bounty. I have often explained it before, but the outrageous statement, that England "receives the worth in sugar of a subsidy of £9,000,000 a year," compels me to repeat it. Why does Sir Thomas Farrer never deal with such an explanation as I have now given? It has been given him often enough, from the days of "Mr. Chamberlain's memorandum" till now. Why does he never attempt to show that I am wrong and he is right?

He goes on to say that there is no more harm to the community in disturbing the natural course of production by bounties—artificially stimulating it in one place and consequently hindering its progress in the rest of the world, thereby making consumers dependent on the success of artificially stimulated crops—than there is in the ordinary process of importing produce under natural conditions. I hope my readers, and his too, can see the difference.

The most-favoured-nation clause, to which matter note fourteen refers, has been dealt with elsewhere (p. 158). I may, however, remark here, as Sir Thomas Farrer

includes France in his list of countries which, he says, will
claim their rights under that clause, that it would be at
least surprising if France, which has always urged a penal
clause in the Sugar Convention, and which has now added
the special bar to objection on most-favoured-nation
grounds, should turn round and claim her rights as a most
favoured nation.

As to the fifteenth note, I think we may safely expect
that the United States will see their great interest in securing the abolition of bounties. In any case they will
never, probably, be exporters of their own production, and
the export of refined sugar is at an end. The penal clause
will, therefore, not affect them. France, Belgium, Austria,
and Brazil—a list given by Sir Thomas Farrer at the end
of his foot-note, to put a finishing touch to the terror of his
readers—will take good care that the Convention shall come
into force. To Brazil it is a matter of life and death that
bounties should cease. Austria has prepared her fiscal
arrangements in full expectation of a general agreement.
Belgium is legislating in the same direction. The French
Government are heartily sick of the big bounty they so
foolishly started in 1884, and will be thankful to have a
good excuse for backing out of it.

The foot-note which comes next contains one of the
largest errors I have yet come across in this book. We
know that Sir Thomas Farrer has pretended that excluding
bounty-fed sugar will reduce supplies and raise price. To
this I have replied that as our markets are open to the
sugars of the world, the visible supply of which is 5,000,000
tons annually, we cannot run short of sugar, and we must
always get it at the price ruling throughout the world. Sir
Thomas Farrer has also refuted his own theory by pointing
out, in another place, that if, which is most improbable, we
should ever exclude French sugar, it would go elsewhere,

and the sugar which it displaced would come here. Of
course that is so. In other words, so long as the world
makes enough sugar for everybody, we shall get as much
as we want, because if we refuse one particular mark we
shall get another instead. But now comes the new and
remarkable fallacy of this particular foot-note. In support
of the old fallacy, Sir Thomas Farrer now urges that " a
small diminution of supply may cause a great increase in
price." Certainly, we have felt it severely in the last
twelve years. The beetroot crop is now more than half
the visible supply of the world. Whenever, therefore, that
crop is deficient, even to the small extent of five to ten per
cent., we now get a big rise in sugar, much to the injury of
the jam trade. We are now dependent on the beetroot
crop, thanks to bounties. But this has absolutely nothing
to do with refusing one particular sugar and taking another
kind instead. Our markets are open to the whole 5,000,000
tons, except, as Mr. Shepheard puts it, when the sugar is
in blue paper wrappers. Sir Thomas Farrer has confused
a diminution in production with a prohibition of blue
paper wrappers.

All notes referring to preceding letters have been
replied to in the replies to the letters.

The next note states that Sir Thomas Farrer is in
favour of free imports. Is the importation of sugar which
receives no bounty to be called a free import, when the
person who desires to bring it here cannot do so without
making the same present to the consumer as that which,
according to Sir Thomas Farrer, the person who brings us
bounty-fed sugar makes. For instance, take the extreme
case in which Sir Thomas Farrer is right in saying that
bounty-fed sugar brings a small present in the sack's
mouth ; that is, when prices are down below natural profit
level. The unsubsidised sugar, if it is to continue to be

H

imported, has then to pay a tax by putting exactly the same present in the mouth of the sack. If it does not do so it has to stop outside. Are these free imports?

In the next note Baron de Worms is blamed because he did not produce Board of Trade returns or other official proofs of the veracity of his figures. Sir Thomas Farrer does not attempt to show that they are wrong, and as he boasts of being very careful about figures we may therefore assume that they are unassailable ; but he nevertheless complains that they are not " proved," *i.e.*, they have not got the official stamp, there is no chapter and verse. This is the official idea of correctness. A figure or a fact is not worth consideration unless it comes out of a Blue Book. There are more figures and facts in the heaven and earth of the commercial cosmos than are dreamt of in Sir Thomas Farrer's philosophy.

The last note contains the stereotyped reply to the question, where should we be if other trades were interfered with by bounties. The reply always is that it would be very nice to have everything given us for nothing. It is a thoroughly senseless reply ; but even in the sugar question there has sprung up a sort of traditional arrangement—that of meeting arguments with cut-and-dried clenchers, which have been found from experience to tell. There never was greater nonsense, and yet the most distinguished men have used it, with grave and learned faces, and a frown at the ignorance of those around them. Of course we all know that a trade will be killed long before it is necessary to give its produce away for nothing. Take boots and shoes. If the cost price is 5s. a pair, it is evident that selling boots and shoes for 4s. 11d. will kill the trade. The difference of a penny makes very little difference to the buyer, but every difference, the difference of life and death, to the seller.

This ends the great and searching criticism of Baron de Worms' speech. An examination of the parts of the speech which have not been touched would enable us to read between the lines with regard to the strength of Sir Thomas Farrer's position. Even his notes have given opportunity for a further considerable damage to it.

As to the note on an extract from Baron de Worms' speech at Liverpool, I will point out, in the first place, that a countervailing duty is not a retaliatory duty. Warding off a blow is not retaliating. A duty on blue paper wrappers is not retaliation. A collecting of a bounty for the benefit of the revenue is not retaliating. "By all means send us your bounty-fed sugar, but let us put it on an equality with other sugar by taking the bounty off before it goes on the market." That is not retaliation, but a method of restoring Free Trade. I could quote a Cobden prize essay wherein that observation is very forcibly put.

As to the Merchandise Marks Act, Sir Thomas Farrer has already dealt with the subject, and so have I. The effect on trade is the same in both cases. The Act is for the purpose of stopping this injurious effect upon trade, not for the purpose of punishing fraud. The assistance of the bounty is neither "unconscious" nor "unintentional," as Sir Thomas Farrer ought, by this time, to be well aware.

The remainder of the note I have already answered (p. 37).

CHAPTER XII.

REPLY TO REPRINT OF CHAPTER XLVIII. ON SUGAR.

From " Free Trade v. Fair Trade."

THIS reprint begins with a note, in which the old attack on the Foreign Office is repeated. That department, it is suggested, has managed to confuse the public on important points, and has tumbled information pell-mell out before the public, without an index, without a summary or digest, and without information as to the state of the trade or the effect of bounties. " Diligent in the service of our sugar planters and refiners ; negligent of all other British interests ; obedient to Spain and Germany, our Government are legislating, and inviting Parliament to legislate in the dark."

Murder will out. Here again, the true reason for this book crops up, with all the bitterness intensified by the long effort to suppress it. The old jealousy between the Board of Trade and the Commercial Department of the Foreign Office bursts forth once more. It is to be hoped that the chief of that department will not consider it his duty also to write a book. He probably has a different view of the nature of his official duties. What are the British interests which the Government are neglecting in this matter? Certainly not those of the consumer, who, as I have repeatedly shown, is already suffering from the effects of bounties, and will suffer severely if they continue. Certainly not those of other industries, which may at any moment be attacked in the same way, if the present opportunity to abolish the bounty system be declined by our Government. Things have gone so far that any such action on the part of the Government, or of Parliament, would be regarded abroad as a distinct invitation to further aggression. The Government is accused of being obedient to Spain and Germany; but if there is any obsequiousness at all it is towards France, that being the country which has for years urged upon the British Government the policy which they have at last had the courage to pursue— the only policy which can restore Free Trade in sugar. As to legislating in the dark, if Blue Books be illumination, with or without indexes, the legislation will come off under a flood of most brilliant light.

Now for the Chapter on Sugar, reprinted from Sir Thomas Farrer's book, " Free Trade v. Fair Trade."

In the first place it must be pointed out that the abolition of bounties has no connection with the controversy known as the Fair Trade controversy. The arguments in the one case are the opposite of those in the other. The Fair-traders desire to meet foreign protective duties by counter protective duties. Those who ask for abolition of bounties desire to abolish the protection of foreigners in British markets, a matter entirely within our own control. We have no power to compel foreign nations to abolish protective duties on British goods; but we have the power to prevent foreign producers from being protected by foreign bounties in our own markets, a process which is equivalent to striking with a differential duty British goods as against freign goods in British markets. The action proposed by Fair-traders would introduce protective duties into this country. The act of abolishing foreign bounties would, on the contrary, restore Free Trade in our own country. Free Trade cannot exist so long as bounties are permitted to give an advantage to the foreigner over the British producer in our home markets.

The chapter begins with a long dissertation on the
"importance of sugar, politically and economically," its
"enormous and increasing supply," and "England's share
as compared with other countries." "It is food;" "it
gives employment;" "it is also raw material;" and "these
are results obtained by free importation." But we have
not yet got free importation. When we do, the benefits
so eloquently stated will be complete. We ask for this
completion of our, at present, imperfect system of free
importation of sugar, but Sir Thomas Farrer energetically
resists the demand. At present, those producers who
receive no bounty are not free to send their sugar to our
markets, unless they are prepared to compete with sugar
which receives a bounty, and, if necessary, to pay out of
their own pockets a sum equivalent to the present which
Sir Thomas Farrer declares that the bounty-fed producer
is making to this country. We ask that free importation
shall become a reality, so that the blessings of a large and
and unrestricted supply shall also become real and permanent. That it is not so now the experience of the
market for the last few years has abundantly shown; and
at the present moment the market is greatly disturbed,
prices are rising rapidly, because a scarcity of sugar is
apprehended. The beetroot crop, it seems, has been
over-estimated, and there is not sufficient cane sugar to
supply the deficiency. The opportunity is seized by
continental speculators to make a corner. There could
not be a better illustration of the injurious influence of
bounties. The consumer is at the mercy of the beetroot
crop, because it has been artificially stimulated, and the
production of cane sugar, consequently, artificially kept
down.

Then follows a dissertation on sugar duties and drawbacks, the "difficulties of European Governments," the

abolition of our sugar duty, and the consequent reduction
in price to the British consumer. This is the real, true
and only reason for the expansion of the confectionery,
jam, and biscuit industries, though Sir Thomas Farrer
wants us to believe that those industries depend for their
prosperity entirely on the unstable foundation of foreign
bounties — a curious contention for a Free-trader to
set up.

The chapter then plunges into the details of the
foreign bounties. As to the German bounty, Sir Thomas
Farrer says it is impossible to gauge its amount with
accuracy. If, however, he had made himself acquainted
with the details of foreign commercial and industrial
statistics he would have found that it can be, and in fact
is, most accurately estimated every year. He explains
that the amount of the bounty depends on the quantity
of sugar which is produced, over and above the quantity
which the beetroot is officially estimated to yield, and on
which the duty is levied. He is not aware that a most
elaborate official report appears annually, giving the
quantity of sugar actually produced, the quantity of roots
worked, and, consequently, the amount of bounty received
by the producers. This chapter was written in 1886, and
he admits that "*under this system the German production
has increased fivefold since* 1871." This is indeed an
admission worth putting in italics. It admits our whole
case. Of course this enormous increase, and the consequent glutting of the markets, which came off in 1884,
has prevented cane sugar from progressing as it otherwise
would have done. So far, on Sir Thomas Farrer's own
admission, the consumer has become dependent, by artificial means, on one particular source of supply, and
therefore on the weather which may happen to prevail in
one particular district of Europe. The sugar market

indicates this fact with ridiculous clearness. It is quite
a new feature in the sugar trade. In the spring, the
lateness of the sowings, owing to prolonged wintry
weather; in the summer, the want of rain, or the too
great abundance of rain; in the autumn, the want of
sun, the prevalence of bad weather, or the too early
approach of winter; all these things are now watched,
in every market throughout the world, with feverish
anxiety. Sudden fluctuations are perpetually taking
place, solely on account of the state of the weather on
the Continent. Can any one say that the consumer is not
becoming absolutely under the thumb of the beetroot
crop? There are many other possible events besides bad
weather which might have a disastrous effect on the
Continental production of beetroot sugar; and where
would the consumer be then? If the producers of cane
sugar were free to expand their production, without fear
of bounty-fed competition, all this dependence on one
crop would be immediately got rid of.

The next statement is equally instructive. "In the
present year (1886) the import of raw sugar from Germany
is decreasing largely, and that of refined sugar increasing."
Why? Because the bounty on refined was, at that time,
made larger in proportion to that on raw. If there was to
be a bounty in Germany that was the natural step to take.
The British refiners have fought the battle for the colonial
producers most loyally from the very first. They have
always maintained the broad principle that if bounties are
to be abolished they must be abolished all round, both on
raw and refined. They know perfectly well that they and
their foreign competitors buy raw sugar at the same price,
and that, therefore, the ridiculous theory that bounties on
raw sugar are an advantage to them is all nonsense. But
now, as I predicted, and as this statement confirms, they

have to fight for their own preservation as well as for the safety of our colonies.

At the end of the same paragraph I find still another statement which admits my case. Sir Thomas Farrer tells us that "*in fact, there has been a glut in the sugar trade, much aggravated by the foolish system of bounties.*" It begins to appear that he would be a valuable witness if we had another Parliamentary inquiry into the state of the sugar industries.

The official report from our Embassy at Berlin, from which Sir Thomas Farrer quotes, says that the German refiners cannot compete successfully with our own. The exports of German refined sugar have, nevertheless, as Sir Thomas Farrer states, enormously increased, and are going on increasing, now that refined sugar is allowed an increased proportion of bounty.

All this helps our case very much, and I am grateful to Sir Thomas Farrer for giving publicity to it. Still more does the quotation from Deputy Gehlert's statement in the Reichstag, in which he bitterly complains that the German sugar industry has been subsidised, during the preceding ten years, to the extent of £7,500,000, and that "in the year of the sugar crisis (1884) the State subsidy amounted to fully £2,000,000." He laments that since it has been thus subsidised it has "*solely in consequence of this stimulus, attained its present dimensions.*" I thought Sir Thomas Farrer always maintained that bounties had nothing to do with our troubles, or those of our colonial friends; and yet he quotes this speech which proves exactly the reverse. Could our complaints be stated more strongly, or with greater authority? He does not even dispute Herr Gehlert's figures, though they have not been checked by the Board of Trade, but accepts them with alacrity.

Austria, he tells us, has also "*felt the recent glut and*

the reaction from the unnatural stimulus." If this be so in countries where bounties still continue, how must the poor commonplace producer fare, who receives no bounty? Sir Thomas Farrer tells us that even in Austria, where there is still a good substantial bounty, " bankruptcies and failures among Austrian sugar makers were notorious during 1884—85." How then does he propose that our colonial producers, unsubsidised and, for his part, uncared for, are to survive? Bounties, Sir Thomas Farrer now admits, have got to such a pitch that they are ruining even the producers who enjoy them, owing to "the unnatural stimulus." And yet he has just brought out a new book to prove that bounties should not be abolished, because it would rob the poor man of his cheap sugar and ruin the jam trade. How is the poor man to have cheap sugar, or jam to be made at all, if not only the unsubsidised, but even, on his own showing, the subsidised industry is being ruined by "the unnatural stimulus?" We are told in one part of the book that cane sugar was never more flourishing —cane sugar which receives no bounty—but now we are told that bounties have been such an unnatural stimulus that even the happy receivers of the bounty, the creators of cheap sugar, are being ruined. How then, if bounties go on, and the same thing recurs, are we to go on enjoying cheap sugar? We are told, in another place, that cane sugar cannot hold its own against beetroot, even if bounties were abolished, because it is "bad sugar," and its makers have no enterprise. Surely this must be a mistake, seeing that cane sugar survived a shock which Sir Thomas Farrer now fully admits to have been so severe, owing to the un-natural stimulus of bounties and the consequently glutted markets, that even the bounty-fed beetroot industry was shaken to its foundations. All that Sir Thomas Farrer is telling us now, in this reprint from his former work, is perfectly true ; but it knocks to pieces everything which he is advancing in the new book. It appears now that he admits and fully appreciates the fact, that the "unnatural stimulus" of bounties culminated, in 1884, in a great glut of sugar, which brought ruin on many of the bounty-fed producers ; and yet he is straining every nerve to prevent the only remedy for an evil which must, *a fortiori*, bring ruin on those who receive no bounty. He is fighting hard to maintain bounties, because their abolition would deprive us of cheap sugar, and all the while he has fully appreciated, and described in graphic language, a crisis which nearly brought ruin on the whole sugar production of the world, and which he himself admits to have been brought about by "the unnatural stimulus of bounties." For more than a hundred pages his readers have been trifled with ; now, at page 107, they are told facts which show that all the rest was fiction. It was an unfortunate moment for Sir Thomas Farrer when he determined to reprint this old chapter. Cheap sugar and a ruined industry cannot co-exist. He admits that the glut caused by the unnatural stimulus of bounties brought the sugar industry within sight of ruin. This is perfectly true ; but, that being so, how is a recurrence of the crisis to be avoided ? Bounties must continue, Sir Thomas Farrer says, or we shall be robbed of our cheap sugar. But he shows that if they do continue we must have another crisis, with ruin staring us in the face. Is this the best and only way of keeping up a good supply of cheap sugar ? Sir Thomas Farrer cannot now possibly escape this dilemma except by frankly admitting that the abolition of bounties is the only way out of it.

Continuing his history of bounties, Sir Thomas Farrer passes on to France. He makes a mistake about her production having increased rapidly. Until the new bounty was started, in 1884, the French production languished owing to the bounty-fed competition of her neighbours. This was the origin of the legislation of 1884, as he correctly proceeds to explain. In a foot-note he quotes, from the *Produce Markets Review*, an estimate of the present French bounty, which exactly tallies with the figures given by Baron de Worms. In the one case he accepts the figures without dispute ; in the other he treats them with every mark of disrespect and suspicion.

Belgium is described as " perplexed by the distress of her sugar interest." This is because the larger German bounty had, as Sir Thomas Farrer so well describes, created a glut by its unnatural stimulus ; also because the new French bounty, one of much larger dimensions, threatened a greater crisis.

Holland does not, as erroneously stated here, " tax her sugar by chemical measurement of the quantity of sugar contained in the juice." Her exports are almost entirely refined sugar, owing to a bounty quite distinct from the bounty on the juice. These, however, are mere errors of detail.

As to Russia, Sir Thomas Farrer's statement clearly shows how a bounty immediately results in large exports, and that, therefore, these exports of foreign sugar, under the bounty systems of the Continent, are purely artificial, and consequently unstable and unreliable. They are, nevertheless, in his opinion, so essential to the well-being of the community that they must be bolstered up and retained at all hazards. Down with Protection, he cries, and long live artificial exports !

The United States produce a certain quantity of sugar, as we have seen already, and we have been told elsewhere by Sir Thomas Farrer that if, at any time, we were to enforce the penal clause against them, we might be shutting out one of our largest sources of supply. Here, however, he uses different language, for he speaks of "their domestic industry, which does not produce a fraction of the amount consumed in the country, and which languishes in spite of Protection." There is a pleasing variety in these two statements, and we must evidently be careful not to accept too readily all the brilliant points of this versatile writer.

Some doubt is expressed by Sir Thomas Farrer as to whether there was, at one time, a bounty on the exportation of refined sugar from the United States. But if he refers to the Blue Books he will find full particulars of the bounty and the method of calculating it. The American bounty furnishes one of the most complete illustrations of the way in which bounties create an artificial trade. Directly it commenced the exports of American refined began, and continued to increase as long as the bounty lasted. By our constant efforts we at last procured its abolition. The exports immediately ceased. A few years afterwards the duties were altered, and this gave the American refiners an opportunity of again mystifying the authorities as to the amount of drawback which ought to be allowed. It should have been 2·40 dollars the 100 lbs., as is clearly proved by calculation from the duty levied on the raw sugar. These calculations are fully stated in the Blue Books. But the American refiners succeeded in getting a drawback of 2·82 dollars, which gives a bounty of 42 cents the 100 lbs., or about 2s. per cwt. The exports immediately recommenced on a large scale, and, as Sir Thomas Farrer says, we were inundated for a time with American refined sugar. Again we agitated, and at last the Secretary to the Treasury at Washington admitted that the drawback was excessive, reduced it to 2·60 dollars, and intimated that it would probably have to be still further reduced; all of which information is in the Blue Books. The immediate result of this reduction was that the artificial exportation languished and speedily ceased, the remaining bounty not being enough to compete with the big European bounties. There could not be a better illustration of the precarious nature of the supply of sugar created by bounties. But, nevertheless, it is this precarious supply that Sir Thomas Farrer contends is so essential to the very existence of our jam trade, and so necessary for the welfare of the consumer. The sudden appearance, and equally sudden disappearance, of an artificial importation of American refined sugar, which amounted, Sir Thomas Farrer tells us, to 10,000 tons a month, and gave a total import, in 1885, of 114,000 tons, is also a most useful illustration of a fact which absolutely annihilates one of Sir Thomas Farrer's most valuable theories. He contends that if we were, by any unlikely chance, ever compelled to enforce the penal clause against some country which, after the conclusion of the Convention, persisted in giving bounties, and thereby endangered the treaty, we should be restricting our supply of sugar and raising the price. I have replied fully to this every time it has been repeated, by pointing out that we have nearly five times as much sugar to choose from as we want, and that therefore we shall always get what we want at the world's price. Sir Thomas Farrer has also destroyed his own theory by showing that prohibition would only result in substituting one sugar for another. But now we have a more practical proof of the fallacy of his original theory.

By the sudden disappearance of the American bounty we suddenly lost a supply of refined sugar amounting to more than 100,000 tons a year. This was exactly as if American refined sugar had been suddenly prohibited. Did we suffer from restricted supplies? Did the unfortunate consumer suddenly find the price of sugar raised a halfpenny a pound? Of course, nothing of the kind happened. We got our sugar from somewhere else, or made it ourselves, and people were quite unconscious that anything had occurred. This finally disposes of Sir Thomas Farrer's fallacy about the effect of prohibition.

It is incorrect to say that Brazil "guarantees a high rate of interest on the capital employed in sugar making." This statement would lead readers to suppose that the sugar producers in Brazil received interest on their capital from the Government. They do nothing of the kind. The bulk of Brazil sugar is produced by persons who have been so occupied for generations before there was any idea of a Government guarantee. This guarantee is only offered with the view of inducing fresh capitalists to embark in large central factories, with all the latest improvements. It is undoubtedly an artificial interference with the course of trade, but it does not touch the bulk of the sugar produced in Brazil, and it is certainly very far removed from the export bounties with which we are now dealing. Brazil is in such a sad state, as to her sugar industry, that she certainly ought to be among the first to promote the abolition of bounties. As Sir Thomas Farrer says, " *ruin is impending over her sugar factories,*" but it is ridiculous for him to ascribe this to the fact that the Government offers to guarantee the interest on the capital devoted to improving the industry. The ruin of the Brazilian sugar industry will be just as much the result of " the glut " caused by " the unnatural stimulus " of bounties, as those other ruins which Sir Thomas Farrer has very properly ascribed to that cause. But how curious it is to see Sir Thomas Farrer here admitting that a large sugar industry like that of Brazil, has " ruin impending over her factories," when, in another place, he contends that it is quite a mistake to suppose that the cane sugar industry is suffering, whether from bounties or any other cause.

He now thinks he has shown that " foreign Governments

are all floundering in the difficulties from which we, by
abandoning all taxation of sugar, have happily emerged."
Does he mean that the ruin which he so frequently
describes, in these last few pages, as impending over
foreign sugar industries, owing to "the glut" caused by
"the unnatural stimulus" of bounties, is escaped by our
home and colonial industries? A reply to this question is
very necessary, for it otherwise puts Sir Thomas Farrer in
a very awkward dilemma. He evidently does not see his
danger, for he goes on to say:—"**Above all, in all these
countries, however much manufacture and export may
have increased, there is great distress among the protected classes. Protection and bounties have produced
their usual results, viz., an unnatural stimulus, and large
immediate profits, followed by a glut, collapse and
ruin.**"

How are we, and our friends in the West Indies,
Mauritius, India, Australia, Natal, and our other friends in
Java, Cuba, Porto Rico, Brazil, Egypt, Manilla, and a host
of other places, to meet this "glut, collapse and ruin," if
even the bounty-fed producers suffer from it? We have
come to a very serious point now, for here we have the
truth stated in most emphatic words—words that even Sir
Thomas Farrer cannot explain away or evade. My
question must be answered, or his whole book becomes
waste paper, always excepting this valuable appendix.
But there is another question even more difficult for Sir
Thomas Farrer to answer, and more destructive to all that
he has hitherto urged. How is the British consumer to
enjoy cheap sugar under the bounty *régime*—a *régime*
which Sir Thomas Farrer says is his only safeguard against
dear sugar—if the result of the bounty *régime* is "collapse
and ruin?" How is the jam maker, whose whole existence,
we are told, depends on the maintenance of bounties—how

is he to get on when this inevitable "collapse and ruin" follows the next inevitable "glut?"

I have wasted my time in answering Sir Thomas Farrer's book; for here it is answered, refuted, and disposed of for me, by this one happy sentence of his, in this most fortunate appendix.

After this, it seems hardly worth while to continue the dreary work of minute criticism; but it must be finished as it was begun, paragraph by paragraph, even at the risk of bathos, after this crushing blow to his book, delivered by the author's own hand.

It seems that this country enjoys a large export trade to Germany, Holland, and Belgium. Sir Thomas Farrer argues that our imports of bounty-fed sugar from those countries are, therefore, desirable, because we pay for them with our exports, and thereby give employment to our workmen in manufacturing the goods exported. He does not say, though he must know, that if we did not import this bounty-fed sugar we should import sugar from elsewhere, and this sugar would be equally paid for by exports. We might import it from our own colonies; in which case we should not only have exactly the same work to do in manufacturing the exports to pay for it, but we should have the further advantage of giving employment to our colonial brethren, and very likely making machinery and a hundred other things for their sugar industry. We might also import raw instead of refined sugar; in which case we should have exactly the same work to do in making exports to pay for the raw sugar; and we should have the additional advantage of employing our own people in refining it, and of making all the necessary appliances for so doing. In either case we should enjoy the still greater advantage, by the abolition of the bounties, of securing the consumer and

I

jam maker against the catastrophe which would result
from the "glut, collapse, and ruin" brought about, as Sir
Thomas Farrer so truly says, by "an unnatural stimulus."
The "collapse and ruin" must inevitably fall first on those
who receive no bounty. From that quarter, therefore, the
consumer and jam maker will first of all lose their supplies.
Whether the bounty will continue long enough to extend
the "collapse and ruin" to the subsidised industry remains
to be seen. But as far as we and our cane sugar friends
are concerned, it is evident from Sir Thomas Farrer's own
showing, that our fate is sealed if bounties continue. He
has also demonstrated with equal clearness that a continuance of the bounties must be followed by dear sugar—an
absolutely certain result of "collapse and ruin" in the
sugar industry.

Now comes Sir Thomas Farrer's great point against
us, up to which all these valuable admissions have been
leading. He accuses us of wanting the same protective
system which has brought "collapse and ruin" on the
sugar industry. And all because we ask for an international Convention for the abolition of bounties, and
for that without which we know, from the experience of
fifteen years of constant negotiations, that no international
agreement can be obtained. It is impossible to procure
from foreign Governments a mutual undertaking to abolish
bounties unless they have full security that their industries
will not have to compete with bounty-fed sugar in the
markets of the contracting powers. For this reason, and
for this reason only, have we urged the adoption of a penal
clause. We have had no ulterior motive. So far from
desiring Protection—with a capital P—we should deprecate
it most strongly. We are far too keenly alive to the
advantages of Free Trade, and to the injury which Protection would inflict on our industry. We have, however,

argued in favour of the penal clause for one other reason, and that is because we are firmly convinced that it is "not only consistent with Free Trade, but positively conceived in the interests of Free Trade." For the last fifteen years we have stated all this, and proved the correctness of our view, in every possible form, whether in the columns of the press, or in "memorandums" addressed to the Board of Trade. Sir Thomas Farrer has seen our statements constantly—more especially recently in the columns of the *Times* in reply to his renewed attacks, and yet he does not hesitate to bring out a new book and again state, what he knows has been contradicted and refuted so often—that we are asking our Government to "imitate the systems of other nations ;" that we are asking for "Protection" and " Retaliation." The abolition of Protection to foreigners on British markets cannot be called Protection to us. That word, when spelt with a capital P, means that the protected industry is placed in an artificial position, by which it is enabled to obtain an artificially high price for its products. That is the position in which foreign sugar producers are placed by means of bounties ; and they obtain the artificial advantage even in our markets. To remove that infraction of Free Trade does not transfer the artificial advantage to us ; it merely removes the inequality and restores Free Trade. And just as the removal of this inequality is not Protection, so also it cannot, by any twisting of language, be called Retaliation.

Then we are told that the interest of the refiner is opposed to that of the West Indian planter, because the one wants raw sugar cheap, and the other wants it dear. This very shallow fallacy has greatly taken the fancy of some people. The answer is that if raw sugar is cheap it is equally cheap to all refiners, and therefore there is no virtue in it from the refiners' point of view, except that people eat more sugar when it is cheap. But that is not Sir Thomas Farrer's point. He thinks we get more profit when raw sugar is cheap. To take a practical illustration, it happens that when raw sugar went down to 10s. a cwt., in the crisis of 1884, the refiners were anything but flourishing. The crisis, as Sir Thomas Farrer has explained, was brought about by a glut of sugar, caused by the unnatural stimulus of bounties, and when the glut came it brought a glut of all kinds of sugar, both raw and refined. There was too much refined sugar, and the refiners had a bad time. It is clear, therefore, that what the refiner wants is not low prices, but only a sufficient margin between the price of raw and refined to pay the cost of refining and leave him a fair profit. All this it would have been supposed that a political economist would have known.

Sir Thomas Farrer then proceeds again to demonstrate that the refining industry is in a most flourishing state. But he forgets how he has just stated that the unnatural stimulus of bounties causes "glut, collapse, and ruin." We know it to our cost ; but because we have stood the shock and braved the storm, we are to be taunted with the accusation of having cried out before we were hurt. We had the foresight to see what was coming many years ago ; and the crisis of 1884—the "glut, collapse, and ruin"—fully justified our anticipations. And yet, for years before that crisis took place, we were met with this same taunt by Sir Thomas Farrer and his friends. He so far admits his error now, that he adds the following reservation :—" Since 1884, however, there is reason to believe that our refiners have been hard hit by the continuance of the German bounties, the new Russian bounties, and the import of refined sugar from America, encouraged by low Atlantic freights and probably also by a system of bounties." Why does he omit to mention the new French bounty, which he says amounts to "from £3,000,000 to £4,000,000 a year," and which so overtops all other bounties that it is bound speedily to bring about another period of "glut, collapse, and ruin," unless all bounties are abolished by mutual agreement? However, it is satisfactory to have at last this tardy recognition from Sir Thomas Farrer that we are not suffering from an altogether imaginary grievance. It is followed by a calm statement, without comment, of the fact that the imports of foreign refined sugar had increased in 1885 to 256,000 tons, to which another 100,000 tons has since been added. The loss of manufacture of 350,000 tons of refined sugar, added to the fact of having to compete against manufacturers who receive an artificial profit, and who can therefore always turn the scale against us, is no insignificant grievance, though Sir Thomas Farrer does his best to minimise it. He kindly gives us his sympathy, but adds that "after all, sugar refining in this country is *at the best* a comparatively small trade." This is in curious contrast with what he says when he wishes to make out that we are very flourishing. Then we are told that the consumption of sugar in this country "represents an annual expenditure of £30,000,000,* or about half the sum which the people of the United Kingdom pay for wheat." It is evident, therefore, that our industry, "at the best," would be a very considerable one, were it not that the foreigner is allowed to be protected on our markets, and consequently gets the lion's share of the trade.

Then our trade is, as usual, compared with the jam trade, under the extraordinary impression—or rather with the view of creating the impression—that the two industries of sugar refining and jam making cannot flourish together in the same country. Why should not the jam maker

---

* Sir Thomas Farrer has only made a mistake of £10,000,000 here.

make as much jam, and as much profit, with British as
with foreign sugar? This dilemma evidently struck Sir
Thomas Farrer, because he adds that, for these "subsidiary
trades, foreign refined sugar has special advantages." We
know that what the Board of Trade says should be always
accepted as indisputable; otherwise, we should have
claimed some slight knowledge of our trade, and been
disposed to smile at so absurd a statement. Every kind
of refined sugar which is made abroad is also made here,
and many other kinds also. As British refined sugar
invariably fetches a higher price than the similar kind of
foreign, it is difficult to understand how it can be shown
that the foreign is preferred. It is a notorious fact that
the best jam makers prefer cane to beet sugar; some will
have it. As the foreign refined is all beetroot, it cannot be
preferred. The point is unimportant, but it serves to
show the kind of straws which are caught at by Sir
Thomas Farrer and his friends.

His next task is to show, by similar methods, that the
West Indian planters are not injured by bounties. He forgets
his recent assertion, that "the unnatural stimulus" of bounties
has brought about "glut, collapse, and ruin." That states
the whole of their case. So long as bounties continue they
must be subject to the recurrence of such a crisis; an anticipation which is quite sufficient to paralyse any industry.

Two mis-statements may be noted in passing, though
they are repetitions of old ones. "In some countries—*e.g.*,
in France—there has in late years been no bounty, and
yet the production increases rapidly." The real facts, as
to France, tell in precisely the opposite direction. The
French production dwindled, owing to neighbouring bounty-
fed competition. To save it from destruction the law of
1884 was passed, giving a heavy bounty to the producers.
The other countries are not specified.

The other mistake is a bad one, showing great ignorance of the rudiments of the subject. We are told that " it is only on the sugar exported that a bounty can possibly be paid, and this is only 700,000 tons out of a total of beet-sugar production of about 2,000,000 tons." Nothing could possibly be more erroneous. Sir Thomas Farrer has explained that the bounty is obtained by producing more sugar than the official quantity which the roots are estimated to yield, and on which the duty is levied. He ought, therefore, to have seen at once that, thanks to the outlet afforded by the drawback system, the producer is always able to obtain from the consumer the full duty-paid value of the sugar. He therefore obtains, owing to the export drawback, the bounty not only on the quantity exported, but also on that which is taken for home consumption.

The allegation that bounties tend to make the consumer dependent on the bounty-fed supply, Sir Thomas Farrer says, " scarcely needs refutation." Unfortunately it is an accomplished fact, and has been so for some years. Three times since 1876 there has been a deficient beetroot crop, and on each occasion there was a rise of 50 per cent. in the price of sugar. That is what we call dependence on the bounty-fed supply, which will become intensified every year that bounties continue. At the present moment we are seeing the progress of what looks very like a corner in sugar, of which Continental operators are the authors. They have discovered that from now till next October they are masters of the situation, and they mean to make us pay for it. Sir Thomas Farrer will therefore find that we are already considerably nearer the " virtual monopoly " which he derides than he was aware of. His refutation comes to nothing, for it is founded on the statement that " much of the supply of beet sugar is not bounty-fed," which I have

just shown to be incorrect.   He also speaks of the "diversified area of production," which makes it as impossible to
create a monopoly as it would be with wheat.   But he has
shown elsewhere that in the course of a very few years the
beet sugar production was increased five-fold, and that this
exaggerated growth, caused by the "unnatural stimulus"
of bounties, ended in "glut, collapse and ruin."   What is
the use of a diversified area of production under such conditions as these, whether the article be sugar or wheat ?   It
is marvellous to hear a great political economist—one who
professes to follow Cobden—use such language as this.

Beet-sugar, he says, has "increased in a much larger
proportion " than cane-sugar ; and yet he brings that fact
forward as his proof that beet is not supplanting cane.   I
have dealt with his figures already, but I note here that he
lays great stress on West India sugar having increased
20,000 tons in three years.   This is indeed introducing
comedy into statistics.   The ordinary fluctuation in the
crop of one island alone would amount to more than that
figure.   All the figures are, however, quite immaterial, now
that we have got the admission that bounties lead to " glut,
collapse, and ruin."   It is only necessary to be noticed in
order to indicate another of the feeble straws to which Sir
Thomas Farrer clings.

There is "no reason to despair of the future of cane-
sugar."   No, none whatever, unless bounties continue, when,
as Sir Thomas Farrer tells us, the " unnatural stimulus "
brings about the necessary consequence of " glut, collapse,
and ruin."   Skill and industry are alone necessary, he
thinks, to enable cane to compete with beetroot.   But who
will be disposed to apply skill, industry, or money on an
industry over which these terrible results of the bounty
system, so well described by Sir Thomas Farrer, are
impending ?

The case and prospects of the cane-sugar producers, who receive no bounty, are "not worse probably at the present moment than those of protected sugar producers in foreign countries." Sir Thomas Farrer does not say on what facts or reasoning this assertion, so apparently contrary to common sense, is based. We ordinary men of business certainly believe that an industry which receives an artificial profit in addition to its natural one, can survive "glut, collapse, and ruin" longer than the industry which depends only on its natural profit, and which is, therefore, heavily handicapped in the race.

The only reason given for this apparent paradox is remarkable. The cane-sugar producers are told that "there has been a general glut, and they, in common with others, have suffered." Sir Thomas Farrer forgets that he has already fully explained the nature of this glut: that it was caused by the over-production of beet-root sugar, arising from the "unnatural stimulus" of bounties. This is not "a general glut," but a particular, special, and artificial glut, brought about, as he says, by an unnatural cause. He cannot deny that so long as the unnatural cause continues the same effects will recur. On what grounds, then, can he possibly maintain that "a share of the American market," coupled with "skill and energy," can overcome the disastrous effects of bounties which he has so accurately described?

Then comes the same argument as that which concluded the question of the refining industry. "The West India interest is a small interest." He does not allude to Mauritius, Natal, India, Australia, or any other sugar-producing British colony. The price of sugar, Sir Thomas Farrer says, has been reduced by bounties to the extent of £5,000,000. A little earlier he told us the reduction was £9,000,000. It does not matter, there is no foundation for either figure. Bounties, as I have shown, have no effect on price except by over-production; and none of the bounty reaches this country until the level of natural minimum profit is passed; and then the least fraction which turns the scale between profit and loss sends the pendulum swinging in the opposite direction.

But following Sir Thomas Farrer's reasoning, where does it lead us? He is, in fact, arguing for the perpetual maintenance of bounties. He says, "They ask us to sacrifice a sum which is more than equal to the whole of their production." He declines to do so; the bounties must continue rather than make such a sacrifice. "The much larger interests of consumers in the United Kingdom" demand it. Bounties, Sir Thomas Farrer says, produce "glut, collapse, and ruin," which is a state of things so beneficial to consumers that it must be maintained at all hazards.

He says the remedy we propose won't do, because it is Retaliation with a capital R; and that all the arguments against Retaliation and Protection apply to our case. I have already proved at great length, and several times that we do not propose either Retaliation or Protection, and that the very sound and conclusive arguments against such a policy, if they have any bearing on our case, are arguments in favour of the proposed remedy. I will not go over the ground again; it is sufficient to state once more the remedy which is proposed, and which Sir Thomas Farrer deliberately and so repeatedly misrepresents, long after his statements have been refuted, and without attempting to meet the refutation. The remedy —the only possible remedy—for bounties, is to get all the bounty-giving countries mutually to agree to abolish them. Every Government that has been in power in this country for the last quarter of a century has been endeavouring to bring this about. We have been parties to a Convention for this purpose, which did not work. We have taken part in many international conferences since that treaty lapsed, in order to bring about a more effective one. We have several times been within an ace of succeeding, and we should long since have done so if we had consented to give the contracting Powers sufficient security that their industries would not have to compete in our markets against bounty-fed sugar. In spite of many high authorities maintaining that such a security would be " not only consistent with Free Trade, but positively conceived in the interests of Free Trade," Sir Thomas Farrer and his friends have hitherto succeeded in preventing this security being given, and consequently all our negotiations have been fruitless. Sir Thomas Farrer and his friends prefer " glut, collapse, and ruin." The present Government have, however, preferred to act on their own opinion, rather than on that of Sir Thomas Farrer. They have obtained a Convention, and have agreed to a penal clause so that the abolition of bounties may be a reality, and not a dead letter. If Parliament agrees to the necessary legislation—preferring Free Trade to the protection of foreigners on British markets—it is almost certain that the penal clause will never be enforced ; all bounties will be at once abolished. That, if it were enforced, there would be no effect on the market and no injury to the consumer, I have already sufficiently proved.

In a footnote the following passage occurs, in reference to the amount of bounty and of countervailing duty, the chapter having been written before the Government had adopted the idea of prohibition :—" The point, however, is immaterial to my argument, since, whatever the duty may be, the price must be raised by the amount stated in the text, or the duty would fail in its proposed effect." Of all the glaring fallacies contained in the book, this is, perhaps, the most extraordinary. Can Sir Thomas Farrer really believe that a duty to countervail a bounty raises the price of the sugar on which it is levied? Two exactly similar sugars are, of course, sold at exactly the same price. But one of them, having received a bounty, is struck with a countervailing duty of 2s. per cwt. Does Sir Thomas Farrer really believe that that sugar immediately fetches 2s. per cwt. more in the market than the other exactly similar sugar which has received no bounty and paid no duty? Or does he believe a still more incomprehensible thing, namely, that because this one particular sugar, which has received a bounty and paid an equivalent duty, has been so treated, therefore the whole of the imports of the United Kingdom have been raised in price to the extent of 2s. per cwt.? He must believe either the one or the other; and each is a *reductio ad absurdum.*

Most of the remainder of this chapter has already been fully answered. There is only one remark requiring notice. Most of the foreign Governments desire to abolish their bounties, Sir Thomas Farrer admits, but adds that they will not do so when they see that we wish it. He must have a very bad opinion both of their common sense and their good feeling. They all accepted our invitation to a Conference ; they have expressed their desire to abolish bounties, and their satisfaction at our Government's efforts to bring about an arrangement. Is there some Board of Trade memorandum which is to make them change their minds at the last moment? Undoubtedly Sir Thomas Farrer will do his best to make the negotiations a failure. It rests with Parliament to say whether his are the views most conducive to the welfare of the country and the progress of Free Trade.

CHAPTER XIII.

REPLY TO STATISTICAL APPENDIX.

THE little appendix containing the latest returns of sugar production appears to have been kindly inserted as assisting in proving our case. Consumption appears to be at a standstill, the increase for the year being only 9,000 tons out of 1,182,618 tons.

The production of cane sugar, it seems, has decreased 98,000 tons, while the production of beetroot sugar has increased by 393,000 tons.

The imports of foreign refined have increased 33,000 tons in one year, and now amount to 350,000 tons a year, a quantity sufficient to keep a good many sugar houses going. The quantity of raw sugar imported, deducting exports, has fallen off 37,000 tons.

This exhausts the information furnished by these figures. Every one of them supports our case. Cane sugar standing still, or rather falling off. Beetroot still increasing by leaps and bounds. It is but a few years ago that the production was under a million tons; now it is nearly three million. It is considerably more than half the visible production of the world. Foreign refined imports have increased enormously in the last few years, and are still increasing.

APPENDIX A.

REPLY TO SIR THOMAS FARRER BY W. P. B. SHEPHEARD,
ESQ., OF LINCOLN'S INN, BARRISTER-AT-LAW.

(*Reprinted from " Sugar."*)

SIR THOMAS FARRER AND THE SUGAR CONVENTION.

THE controversy, so long waged in the Blue Books between
former officials of the Board of Trade and the representatives of the sugar industry, has been shifted to the columns
of the *Times*. Sir Thomas Farrer appears in his accustomed *rôle* as champion of foreign Protection ; he sees a
British industry restricted by unfair trading, and he denounces the means taken to remove the restriction. Sir
Thomas Farrer should start an "Unfair Trade League,"
and proclaim himself the president. We are afraid the
foreign bounties have destroyed some economic reputations
as well as closed our sugar refineries. How is it possible
to reconcile Sir Thomas Farrer's bold advocacy of one of
the worst forms of Protection with his protestations in
favour of Free Trade? And yet the Cobden Club has
endorsed Sir Thomas Farrer's views in a leaflet. Surely
these latter-day Free Traders have got adrift ! They no
longer appeal to the well-known principles upon which
Free Trade was established ; on the contrary, Sir Thomas
Farrer proclaims himself a patriot rather than a Free Trader.
As a Free Trader, he denounces bounties ; as a patriot, he
approves them. We can only explain Sir Thomas Farrer's
position on this bounty question by recalling to mind
Cobden's warning "that there were many heads which

could not comprehend and master a proposition in political economy."

Now, the proposition in political economy which Sir Thomas Farrer appears to get into confusion about happens to be the very one upon which the whole fabric of Free Trade was built up. The early English economists based their advocacy of Free Trade upon the advantage of leaving to natural causes the determination of the channels of industry and trade. The great political expositors of Free Trade succeeded in overthrowing the Protectionists by the appeals they made to the people against the interference of governments with the natural course of trade. What are the principles relied upon by Cobden in the press of the controversy in which he was engaged? He says—"We do not seek Free Trade in corn primarily for the purpose of purchasing it at a cheaper money rate; we require it at the *natural* price of the world's market; whether it becomes dearer with Free Trade, or whether it becomes cheaper, it matters not to us, provided the people of this country have it at its natural price, and every source of supply is freely opened, as nature and nature's God intended it to be; then, and then only, shall we be satisfied."

Here was the primary idea which, vindicated by the more abstruse science of political economy, carried conviction to the minds of the people. To it is due the impulse which destroyed Protection in this country, and it is the same impelling conviction which, notwithstanding the ill-conceived efforts of Sir Thomas Farrer, will bring about the cessation of the bounties. How is it that so much misconception exists as to the principles involved in the discussion of this bounty question? To read Sir Thomas Farrer's letters which appeared in the *Times* of the 5th of September and 3rd of October, one would suppose that the Government were upon the eve of giving effect to some

great Protectionist interference with the natural order of
things in our sugar trade. As the full text of the Sugar
Convention appears in our present issue, our readers can
judge for themselves as to its provisions. We search in
vain for any semblance of Protection; for any form of retaliation; or for what Sir Thomas Farrer is pleased to
designate as "the first step openly taken by the British
Government in the direction of commercial retaliation and
restriction—the first official abandonment of the policy of
free imports."

We hardly know how to do justice to the discursive and
loosely-reasoned statements of this latter-day Free Trader.
We cannot, with the sublime generosity of the *Times*, afford
space to reproduce the letters. Yet to sift out the leading
propositions brings into cruel juxtaposition the most con-
flicting assertions: " Foreign bounties are very bad things "
—" The compensatory advantages to us are very great "—
" Our true policy is to let foreign nations take care of themselves"—" They, in their folly, offer us a free gift"—"These
Sugar Bounties are uncertain and, in their origin at least,
unintentional "—"To exclude bounty-fed sugar must be to
deprive the consumer of sugar which he now enjoys." Is
it necessary to string together any more of these miscellaneous apothegms? We will do that which Sir Thomas
Farrer has shirked doing; he knows the value of generalities: *dolosus versatur in generalibus*. We will endeavour
to convert his generalities into specific propositions. Here
they are: (1) Foreign bounties on export are a benefit to
us as a nation; (2) An international agreement for the
abolition of bounties involves a return to Protection; (3)
The exclusion of imports of bounty-aided sugar is a violation of the most-favoured-nation Article; (4) The prohibition of imports of bounty-aided sugar is a restriction on
imports of sugar.

We cannot reduce to any intelligible proposition Sir Thomas Farrer's attempted exposition of the effect of bounties on prices. The relation of bounties to market values is the *pons asinorum* in the political economy of the question. Few thinkers get across this bridge, and Sir Thomas Farrer is not one of them.

Taking, then, the propositions into which we have endeavoured to summarise all that is material to the controversy in Sir Thomas Farrer's letters, we proceed to deny them *seriatim*. We join issue with Sir Thomas Farrer on the first, and assert that foreign export bounties are no benefit, but an injury, to us as a nation, because they are a violation of Free Trade.

The chain of economic reasoning supporting our contention is as follows :—There are two forms of Protection, one by a differential and hostile tariff, whereby States exclude or restrict the entry of foreign competing labour products into their own markets : this is defensive Protection. The other, by means of export bounties whereby States exclude or restrict the entry of labour products competing with their own into foreign markets : this is aggressive Protection.

But how exclude or restrict? We reply, by the operation of a differential price. Let the United Kingdom be the common market for labour products of our own and other States. Our policy of Free Trade opens our market to all competitors, without favour or restriction to any. This policy rests on the unassailable conviction that the natural advantages of each competitor are the best elements for determining the course of competition. Let the competitors be A, B, C, D, up to X. Each, under a Free Trade *régime*, relies solely on the natural market price to recoup cost of production. But directly A, B, and C get an export bounty, they receive both the market price ($\pounds x$)

J

and the cash bounty ($£y$); but all the other competitors only receive the market price ($£x$). Therefore, there is a constant differential element in price operating against all competitors without bounties.

Let us compare this variation from the pure Free Trade competition of natural advantages with the variation which would follow the imposition of Protective tariff duties. Competitors A, B, C, D, up to X, having been admitted to our market at one and the same rate of, or without payment of, duty, are now, with the exception of (say) A, B, and C, subject, by our assumption, to a duty of $£y$.

Then all competitors, except A, B, and C, get the market price, $£x—£y$ (the duty); whilst A, B, and C receive the undiminished market price, $£x$. The differential element in each hypothetical case is the same, viz., $£y$.

For the sake of clearness, we will tabulate the effects of these two forms of Protection :—

Under Protective Duty System.

A, B, and C (duty-free competitors)
 receive market price   -   -   - $£x$
Other competitors (subject to duty $£y$) $£x—£y$

Differential fiscal advantage to A, B,
 and C   -   -   -   -   - $£y$

Under Export Bounty System.

A, B, and C (bounty-aided competitors)
 receive market price ($£x$) and
 bounty ($£y$)   -   -   -   - $£x+£y$
Other competitors   -   -   -   - $£x$

Differential fiscal advantage to A, B,
 and C   -   -   -   -   - $£y$

It is clear, then, that the economic mischief is in both cases identical. Moreover, it is the very mischief Free Trade was instituted to prevent—viz.: The mischief of competition being restricted by State intervention instead of developed by the free play of natural advantages, and the consequent result of the inferior and, therefore, more costly production ousting the superior and, therefore, cheaper production.

It is obvious that, so far as the displacement of natural channels of industry is concerned, foreign bounties on export operate directly on our own country. A fugitive and precarious advantage temporarily enjoyed by our consumers of to-day is no compensatory advantage, as Sir Thomas Farrer would make out, for the permanent loss of the work and wages incidental to a great industry, and for the transfer to the consumers of to-morrow of the burthen of the bounty-aided and, therefore, inferior and more costly zone of production. He says the consumers of the United Kingdom pay £30,000,000 annually for their sugar. At a wage rate of £60 a year, this sum represents work and wages for 500,000 men. The tendency of bounties is to shift production from the cane-sugar zone, in which British interests lie, to the beet-sugar zone—the one gains what the other loses. This is clearly indicated by the statistics of imports. Instead of some five per cent. of the total imports of sugar to this country being beet sugar, as was the case during the ten-year period preceding the bounty system (1852 to 1861), over 60 per cent. is now the percentage of beet sugar.

Now we desire to be perfectly fair to our opponent, and at once admit that he does not wish to urge that the substitution of the sugar from one zone for that of another by arbitrary means is a benefit, but that the bounty which effects the substitution is a benefit.

But now comes the difficulty of our opponent's position. Every British or national industry is of some value to this country. But its value, we allow, is never esteemed great enough to make it worth our while to support it by State aid against the natural forces of world-wide competition. We leave it to its own inherent power in reliance on its natural advantages to stand or fall. We do not impose restrictions on it; we do not favour it. But ought any foreign State be allowed to impose restrictions? What is a bounty unless it is a restriction on competition? It is, in other words, the price paid by a foreign State to us for the purpose of restricting the competition of a British industry. France gives us a bounty in order to stop the competition of our refiners. The cash bounty is the advantage which Sir Thomas Farrer makes the most of. But the nation has its share of the £30,000,000 worth of work and wages, represented by our sugar consumption, subjected to an annually-increasing diminution.

If the officials of the Board of Trade are to stand behind a counter in order to sell British industries to foreign governments, we must have a better price than some "uncertain amount of bounty" for such an industry as that of sugar. On the one side of the account is the "uncertain bounty" derived from the "folly" of foreign governments. On the other side of the account is diminished and diminishing work and wages. In short, for a mere donation, not renewable except at option of foreign donor, we are selling the permanent wage annuities of successive generations of our working classes.

Every four tons of sugar consumed per annum represents just £60 per annum to labour. Is it beneficial to the whole nation to sell permanent annuities of £60 for an uncertain donation of say £20 per annum.—that is, taking the bounty as high as £5 per ton—in other words, to sell the work and wages incidental to the production of every four tons of sugar, say £60, for the uncertain bounty of from £2 to £5 per ton ?

When we perceive the effect of bounties on our labour interests, we are not surprised to learn that it was due to the pressure of the great Trades Unions of this country upon the government, at a critical period in the recent Conference, that the absolute exclusion of bounty-fed sugar was agreed to. We should be false to our faith in Free Trade if, like Sir Thomas Farrer, we could bring ourselves to believe that, under any other *régime* than that of Free Trade, our consumers of sugar would realise for their purchasing power the utmost value the world was capable of affording them ; or that the production of sugar could ever be settled on any better basis than its natural basis, as established by the salutary process of evolution, ever tending to secure the survival of the fittest.

But Sir Thomas Farrer wishes, apparently, the inference to be drawn that the greater the import of foreign bounty-aided sugar, the greater the demand on our labour for goods in exchange. He somehow fails to discern that every unit of wealth produced within our own zone of production is the reciprocal demand for another unit in exchange. Hence if the natural course of things happened to enable us both to produce the whole £30,000,000 of sugar and the goods for which it was exchanged, the national labour would operate on both sides of the exchange, instead of one side only, as in the case suggested by Sir Thomas Farrer. Therefore there is no *primâ facie* advantage in additional imports of foreign sugar, on the grounds that they stimulate exports of British goods. Passing from this digression, we assert that economic reasoning leads us step by step to the absolute conclusion that foreign bounties are a permanent injury to the nation as a whole.

The more advanced economic thinkers have always supported what is termed "Free Trade," on the grounds that it eliminated nationalities from the area of production by extending the principle of the sub-division of labour over the whole available area of production, and that the most effective sub-division of labour was always the direct result of the play of natural, as opposed to arbitrary or State-created forces.

No economic thinker ever confused the great principles of Free Trade with the questions involved in the comparative advantages of indirect and direct taxation. But Sir Thomas Farrer, as well as other leaflet writers for the Cobden Club, seems to assume that any import duty is a violation of Free Trade. No one denounced this confusion of thought more persistently than Cobden. Speaking at a contested election for the City in 1843, he said : " We have said thousands of times that our object is not to take away the Queen's officers from the Custom House, but to take those officers away who sit at the receipt of custom to take tithe and toll for the benefit of peculiar classes."

In spite of true economics, and of Cobden's own warning, the latter-day Free Traders of the Cobden Club have so warped the minds of the working-classes that they absolutely declare, by their authorised representatives, in favour of absolute prohibition of bounty-aided sugar, rather than of the mere transfer of the bounties into our revenue by a countervailing duty. We do not quarrel with the decision ; its advantages in point of simplicity and effectiveness are great.

We now come to the second proposition : " That an international agreement for the abolition of bounties involves a return to Protection." We join issue on this, and

assert that the Convention is simply the restoration of Free
Trade.   How can Protection, which is national exclusive-
ness, ever be involved in an international agreement?   If
all States now giving bounties were by independent action
to abolish them to-morrow, would the result be a return
to Protection?   Of course not!   Then why should an
international agreement to effect the same result be
regarded as a violation of Free Trade?   But the international agreement was to be secured only by the equitable
and salutary provision that any nation standing out should
not retain a differential advantage over the adherents of a
sounder policy.   Its bounty-aided products are excluded ;
but it cannot complain—bounties are voluntary, and *volenti
non fit injuria*.

On the third proposition we likewise join issue.   We
deny that the prohibition of imports of bounty-aided sugar
is contrary to the provisions of the most favoured nation
Article in our commercial treaties.   We agree with the
representatives of Spain and Germany, at the recent International Conference, that export bounties themselves are
a direct violation of the spirit and intention of that Treaty
Article.   We have already demonstrated that the effect of
a bounty on international competition is exactly identical
with the effect of a differential duty.   The most favoured
nation Article is a provision directed against all differential
treatment (*inter se*) of the imports of foreign States into
our ports.   If any one of these foreign States can be
permitted to vary in its own favour, by means of export
bounties, its competing position with other foreign States
on our markets, then the very mischief which the favoured-
nation Article was intended to prevent immediately arises.
This is a sufficient reply to Sir Thomas Farrer's bare and
unsupported assertion.   But it may be necessary at some
future time to discuss this point more fully in its bearing

on international law. It is obvious, however, that unless some positive action is taken against imports of bounty-aided goods, each nation is almost bound to secure itself in its full enjoyment of the most-favoured-nation Article by giving whatever bounty it may find necessary to restore the equality of competition which was the object of that Article.

We now come to the last proposition, that " prohibition of imports of bounty-aided sugar is a restriction on imports of sugar." This we deny, and, on the contrary, say that it is simply the prohibition of bounties, not of sugar. It is the substitution of sugar without bounty for sugar with bounty. If sugar wrapped in blue paper were excluded, whilst that wrapped in white paper were admitted, there would be no restriction on imports of sugar, but simply of the blue-paper wrappers. We secure the Free Trade wrapper for our sugar by excluding the Protectionist wrapper of a bounty.

In conclusion, we regret that Sir Thomas Farrer should have sought to damage a great national industry ; that he should have advanced theories which assail the very foundations of Free Trade ; that he should champion the interests of foreign Protectionists. But the Convention is unassailable ; it will be ratified by Parliament, and in-augurate that *régime* of " Free Trade and no Protection " so long in abeyance as regards our great Home and Colonial sugar industry. Under this *régime*, each and every nation will once more enjoy the full advantages of its respective natural resources for the production of sugar.

APPENDIX B.

SIR,—The letter in your columns of yesterday on the subject of the Sugar Bounties Convention from Sir T. H. Farrer will be read with the attention to which anything coming from the pen of the late permanent chief of the Board of Trade is naturally entitled. That the Convention should be as gall and wormwood to him will cause no surprise to those who have for years past watched the intense —I had almost said the acrimonious—zeal which he has displayed in preventing anything whatever being done to bring about a cessation of bounties.

Sir Thomas Farrer says—"Bounties, like protective duties, are bad things; but this is not the way to get rid of them." Perhaps he then would explain how he would get rid of them. The doctrine was preached many years ago that foreign Governments, if left alone, would abolish bounties themselves. This has been tested for twenty-five years, with the result that the policy of giving bounties, so far from being abandoned, has been largely extended. Your correspondent taunts the Government with going cap in hand to foreign Powers, but this has been rendered necessary by the commercial policy of this country for the last half-century. Would he have wished the Government to follow the example of Spain, who, when she wished us to reduce the duties on her wines, did not come to us cap in hand, but imposed 30 per cent. extra duty on English goods going into Spain? Although this measure was successful, it was one which Sir Thomas Farrer would hardly wish to see imitated by our Government.

Your correspondent speaks more than once of cheap bounty-fed sugar in such a way as to lead anyone who was excessively ignorant into the belief that bounty-fed sugar is cheaper than non-bounty-fed sugar. I need hardly say that this is not, and never can be, the case, either with or without the Convention. Sugar, bounty-fed or otherwise, will sell at the same price in the same market relatively to its value at all times.

Sir Thomas Farrer fears that we may possibly under the Convention be prevented from buying sugar from the United States and Sweden. The United States produce less than 200,000 tons, and consume more than 1,200,000 tons, so that they are not likely to have any surplus sugar to send us for some time to come. Sweden may or may not export sugar, but if she does the quantity is so small that it finds no place in any published returns available to those interested in the sugar industry. He also throws out some doubts respecting France, Austria, Brazil, and Denmark. But the quantities of sugar we receive from France and Austria are comparatively small, while from Denmark we receive none at all. But as regards Austria and Brazil, there can hardly be a doubt as to their adhesion to the Convention, and I believe it will be found that France will also come in. But even if these Powers remain outside, the total amount of sugar available for export from France and Austria is hardly one-twentieth of the world's supply, and the effect of excluding their sugar would consequently be absolutely inappreciable upon the price. Moreover, it must be borne in mind that it is only sugar receiving a bounty that will be boycotted. Brazil does not give a bounty, so that her sugar would in no case be shut out;

and as for France and Austria, these Powers are solemnly committed by their declarations in the Protocol to the policy of suppressing bounties.

Further, a complaint is made that the process of ascertaining whether sugar is bounty-fed or not, "is one of the most perplexing technical questions which financial necessities have ever inflicted upon legislators—a question which all the cleverest experts of the ablest Governments have hitherto been unable to solve." But this is a complete mistake. It is quite true that some of the authorities of the Board of Trade, while Sir T. Farrer was its chief, professed to find great difficulty in ascertaining whether bounties were granted or not in certain countries, but no such difficulty has been found by foreign officials, and the countries giving bounties are perfectly well known not only to them, but to all concerned in the industry. I should be sorry to think that the officials of our own Board of Trade, under their late chief, were lacking in intelligence as compared with foreign officials; but if Sir T. Farrer, when alluding to "the cleverest experts of the ablest Governments," meant to refer to his own department, there is, I fear, no other conclusion to be arrived at.

Further, some alarm is expressed at the possible effect the Convention may have in preventing our colonies from giving bounties, and that we may have to boycott their sugar. It is really quite amusing to see Sir Thomas Farrer posing as the friend of our colonial sugar industries, and professing alarm on their account; but I am happy to be able to reassure him. The colonies are included in the Convention, and all their sugar industries are fully represented upon the British and Colonial Anti-Bounty Association, of which I am the chairman, and I am in a position to say that there is not the slightest fear of our having to boycott any colonial sugar whatever.

It is not for me to say whether Sir T. Farrer's allusions to Baron Henry de Worms are in good taste ; but I do know that those who are practically acquainted with the subject are best able to appreciate the great ability shown by the Baron in overcoming the difficulties he has had to contend against—difficulties which Sir T. Farrer, in spite of his condemnation of bounties, has certainly not assisted to remove. I believe the services rendered by Baron de Worms will be more generously appreciated by an unprejudiced public, as I know they are by our sugar-growing colonies and the home industries connected with sugar.

I am, Sir, your obedient servant,

N. LUBBOCK, Chairman of the British
and Colonial Anti-Bounty
Billiter House, Sept. 6.　　　　Association.

SIR,—I had hoped that the Sugar Convention might now have been allowed to rest until the House of Commons discussion takes place, when I venture to say the public will have a better opportunity of learning the truth about the bounty question than by reading Sir Thomas Farrer's one-sided and incorrect statements.

I cannot claim your indulgence to afford me space to answer in detail the three columns of statements and arguments occupied by Sir Thomas Farrer's letter in *The Times* of the 3rd inst. I would, however, ask your permission to make a few general remarks in reply.

Sir Thomas appears to maintain :—

(1) That if bounties are abolished sugar will become dearer.

(2) That bounties are bad things, but foreign protective

duties are worse, and that as we do not remedy the one evil we must not remedy the other.

(3) That bad as bounties are for the general industry of the world, they are good for us.

(4) That by stopping bounty-fed sugar " we put a stop to those manufactures of our own which we now export in order to pay for the bounty-fed sugar."

My reply is as follows :—

(1) The highest authorities upon sugar both in Germany and England are of opinion that if bounties are abolished the value of sugar will not be raised. Ample reasons could be given for this if space permitted.

(2) We do not interfere to get rid of protective duties abroad, because we cannot do so effectively. If Baron de Worms could bring about a mutual agreement among foreign Powers to abolish protective duties in the same way as he has brought about an agreement to abolish bounties, he would undoubtedly have a double claim on the gratitude of his countrymen.

(3) Sir Thomas assumes that bounties have reduced the price of sugar, apparently £5 per ton, judging from a quotation he gives from a report of Mr. Giffen's. It is not impossible that at some particular moment, as in 1884, sugar was £5 per ton below the price it would have been at had bounties never existed, just as in 1877 the price was probably £10 per ton higher from the same cause; but the idea that sugar has been permanently at a price anything like £5 per ton below what it would have been but for bounties is quite preposterous. At the present moment I am confident that there is no depreciation due to bounties. But even if Sir Thomas could show some slight gain in price, he has an annual loss of from £3,000,000 to £4,000,000 to set against it.

(4) It surely seems hardly necessary to point out that if bounties are abolished, manufactures of our own will be equally exported to pay for non-bounty-fed sugar.

Bounties are bad things, says Sir Thomas Farrer, but they are better than Free Trade. Is not Sir Thomas "masquerading as a Free-trader?"

I remain, Sir, your obedient servant,

North Berwick, Oct. 6.   N. LUBBOCK.

APPENDIX C.

SIR,—The members of the London Workmen's Anti-Sugar Bounty Association have read with some pain, and no little curiosity, Sir Thomas H. Farrer's letter of three columns upon the Sugar Convention which appeared in *The Times* of the 3rd inst.

It pained us to witness so much zeal for the maintenance of the bounties. In a letter that appeared as recently as last month, and upon previous occasions, Sir Thomas Farrer, without reserve, condemned the bounties as bad things. He then only exhorted the masters who were being ruined by the bounties, and their skilled *employés* in danger of finding themselves levelled down to the condition of day labourers, to bear patiently, as inevitable, the great injury which attends this pernicious system. But now he defends it by special pleading; and, notwithstanding his social position and official experience, we feel constrained to ask, "Who is this that darkeneth counsel by words without knowledge?"

There is a great deal of padding in the letter of the 3rd inst., intended to gain the interest and the votes of many who are not acquainted with the sugar trade and the history of the origin and effect of the bounties. The letter before us contains much that is true, and much that is new, but unfortunately "that which is true is not new, and that which is new is not true."

Sir Thomas Farrer seems to go much further in this attempt to discredit the labourers of the Government than he has ever done before ; and it appears to us that "more is meant than meets the ear." It is not until we have nearly arrived at the bottom of the first column that we find anything worthy of notice. After an allusion in very bad taste to Messrs. Kelly and Peters, with whom our association has no connection whatever, but who have certainly worked hard for our cause, and persevered for many years, and, after a sneer at Baron de Worms and at Messrs. Martineau and Lubbock, we come to the assertion that foreign bounties can only injure the West Indian sugar growers and the British sugar refiners "by making sugar cheaper to us all than it would otherwise be, and the abolition of the bounties can benefit them only by making it dearer to us all."

There is a studied injustice in this statement which we hope the majority of fair-minded men will perceive. The object of the Convention, with which every State that attended it agreed in principle, is to put an end to an artificial price that is destroying a home industry. Neither the British public that consumes, nor the jam boilers and kindred trades, the makers of brewers' substitutes, &c., have any right to receive the inducement of the bounties to patronise the foreigner. The sugar can be refined in many parts of the United Kingdom certainly as well and as cheaply as in any other country, and therefore the difference caused by the bounty is not a question of the cost of production. It is simply a bribe. We are not asking for any "benefit" when we demand that this premium shall be defeated by the decision at which the majority of the Convention has agreed to.

Although the bounty is only one farthing per pound,

it has been found to be sufficient to nearly destroy the home industry of sugar refining, and to make moribund what still survives of it. Our association includes all the *employés* of the sugar refineries that have not closed their gates in this immense gathering of population and consumers in the whole valley of the Thames between Windsor and Woolwich. Our name unfortunately is not "legion," for only four refineries remain at work. Our association was formed about twelve months ago, when five refineries were open, and every man in them eagerly joined us. There are only four at work now, and some of our members have for months been depending upon precarious employment about the docks, losing probably half their time. Others, who once earned their 30s. and 35s. per week, are now hiring barrows at one shilling per week, and trying to sell toys and other things in the streets. When we see this outcome of the bounty system, producing so much suffering among skilled and industrious citizens, we feel bound to declare that there is "something rotten" in it. The professors, who regard it from a very different point of view, do not admit this undeserved suffering into their calculations. We can point out to them that there are more things in Heaven and earth than are dreamt of in their philosophy. It cannot be worth while, for the sake of the saving of one farthing per pound below the true cost of production, to suffer an independent honest industry, that asks no favour, to be destroyed. Probably there is no other business in the world that sails so close to the wind. It is worked by the exercise of the most rigid economy, and by the rapid turnover of a very large capital. It is easy to understand that one farthing per pound advantage granted by foreign exchequers to foreign competitors must speedily put an end to sugar refining in this country.

K

The Government has certainly been right in counting
the cost of the loss of this manufacture to the community—
the loss of costly plant, and the suffering of working men,
and balancing these losses against the almost imperceptible
eleemosynary saving in the domestic use of sugar, or in
its employment in trades that have no right to, and no
occasion for, this advantage. The bounties perhaps, on the
average, reduce the price of sugar one farthing per pound
below the true cost of production. Perhaps they do not
affect the price quite so much. Some portion of the
premium, after underselling the British refiners, may remain in the foreigners' pockets. But certainly this premium
cannot permanently affect the price by more than its own
value. It has not got the purse of Fortunatus. Reversing
this rule, if we succeed in defeating the bounties by the
agreement of the Convention, the price cannot remain
higher than the point from which these meddling bounties
had depressed it, whatever may be the temporary effect of
speculation.

Sir T. H. Farrer may be an excellent theorist, but we
do not accept his *ipse dixit* upon the working and the
fluctuations of markets, for he is not a merchant. We see
no reason why we should hesitate to do away with an evil
which has been condemned by Mr. Gladstone in un-
measured terms as well as by the leaders of the party now
in office.

Our opponents seem to treat us as if we had no existence. But, thanks to the Government, we have not been
forgotten.

We wish our fellow citizens to reflect and judge what
would be now the general opinion about the bounties if
the refining of sugar had been localised in one particular
portion of the United Kingdom, instead of being distri-
buted all over England and Scotland. If, for instance, the

whole body of masters and men, with their capital and their acquired skill, were already ruined and suffering, or in imminent jeopardy of bankruptcy and the workhouse. If these were all concentrated in such a condition within one of the four provinces of Ireland, so as to arrest the attention and the sympathy of everybody — especially if it were obvious to the least observant that there were no other available manufacturing employments in the province except agricultural labour—we might feel sure that no theories would hinder us from applying a remedy.

We desire that practical men capable of taking large views and of considering every interest should deal with a great question like the bounties. We do not wish it to be left in the hands of experts. The great Richard Cobden, who introduced and negotiated the French Commercial Treaty, would never have adopted Sir T. H. Farrer's academical views of this international question. The baronet's letter would have us believe that we gain customers for British manufactures by giving a preference to bounty-fed sugar. This is quite an incorrect argument, because the bribe of a farthing per pound cannot appreciably increase the consumption, and our custom is only transferred from sugar producers in other parts of the world, who would not take less, and might very likely take more of our commodities in exchange for their raw material. It is for our advantage that the cultivation of cane sugar throughout the breadth and circumference of the tropics should be encouraged by the abolition of the bounties. We should then be less affected by the local accidents of a failure of crops, and a great deal more employment would be given to shipping and to our docks, and to all other waterside interests.

It is obvious that it would be better for the whole community if the trade were restored to its natural channels by the destruction of the bounties.   The majority of the Convention has agreed to a certain course, and those who still hesitate will find it necessary to come in to the agreement, as they cannot do without the great British market.

Touching upon the question of markets, we come to the last argument in the letter before us which seems to us to be worthy of notice, and that is the comparison between retaliation to induce other countries to practise Free Trade with us, and the destruction of bounties by countervailing duties or by exclusion.   The difference is very obvious. Retaliation fails because we do not control the markets of other countries.   We double the injury to ourselves by increasing the cost of what we could import for our own use, and we appear to have become converts to the principles of Protection, which we strengthen by our example. On the other hand, what our Government has joined the majority of the Convention in agreeing to is simply to prevent the sale of bounty-fed sugar at an artificial price which is unjust to a great interest in our own market, which we absolutely do entirely control ; and as no other sugar-producing country can get along without this market it is quite certain that the object of killing the bounties must be accomplished.

Yours respectfully,

GEORGE SHUTE,

Member of the Executive of the London Workmen's Anti-Sugar-Bounty Association, representing all the operatives of the sugar refineries now remaining at work in London and in London suburbs, viz. :—Messrs. H. Tate and Sons, Thames Sugar Refinery, Silvertown, Essex ; Messrs. A. Lyle and Sons, Plaistow Wharf Sugar Refinery, Silvertown, Essex ; Messrs. D. Martineau and Sons, St. George's East, London ; Messrs. L. Cowan and Sons, Hammersmith, London, S.W.

Thames Sugar Refinery, Silvertown, Essex, Oct. 6.

Sir,—The members of the London Workmen's Anti-Sugar Bounty Association cannot help remarking with wonder and with some amusement Sir Thomas H. Farrer's numerous letters that rapidly follow each other in their efforts to discredit the results of the Convention with which every country that was represented agreed in principle.

These letters, which a great authority that before 1886 condemned the bounties now considers to be "weighty," are not like those of "Junius," for a peep at which in country towns the post-boys sometimes nearly lost their saddle-bags. We suspect there will be few readers of these dreary pro-sugar-bounty letters except workmen and their employers, who, like ourselves, feel that our future welfare depends upon the success that has been achieved by the Government.

We recommend everybody who feels the least interest in this important international question to read what Baron de Worms will say on the 1st of November at the banquet to be given to him at Greenock. It is probable that on this occasion he will reply to and demolish all the objections that are being raised to the agreement that has been signed.

Sir Thomas Farrer is still harping on this subject to-day, and, like other theorists, is full of prophecy. He avoids the question whether or not it is right to allow the foreign, State-nursed, protected sugar to be sold at an artificial price in our own home market and to acquire the monopoly of it by beating the home industry to the ground. Sir Thomas knows that this is not right, and that it is not free trade. We are masters in our own market, and we ought to defeat the injustice of the bounties which ruin fellow-citizens It is quite absurd to compare this to a war of tariffs and a policy of retaliation. We have no control over foreign markets. We can only

retaliate by punishing ourselves, making the raw materials
for our manufacturers and the food their hands live upon
unnaturally dear. What we principally take in exchange
from abroad are raw materials and food. We should also
seem to have become converts to protection, and would
strengthen its principles by our unlucky example. The
professors of the Cobden Club ought to know better than
throw sand in the eyes of the public, who are too busy to
think these questions out. These doctrinaires are, in fact,
prostituting a great name and a great memory—the
memory of a statesman of wide sympathies, who would have
taken the part of his countrymen in the circumstances we
are in. It is unjust to use the authority of Cobden's name
to make people believe that defeating bounties has anything whatever to do with the puerile trifling of fair-traders
and retaliators.

Until recently, Sir Thomas Farrer always admitted
that "bounties are bad things." Why, then, hesitate to
destroy them? Why should we be afraid to strike while
the iron is hot, and while the majority of the Convention
will sign the agreement? We know that it must be necessary for the countries that have not yet signed to follow
suit. They agree with us in principle, and are only pro-
crastinating in order to conciliate the vested interests into
which the rotten system of bounties has, unfortunately,
attracted much capital and much trained skill, causing
ultimately a lamentable waste. Out of consideration for
this unhappy outcome of a foolish policy, the bounty-
paying countries are getting three years' grace. In the
meanwhile they will be taught that they have no alternative
but to follow the action of the majority and submit to the
inevitable. They cannot get along without the great
British market. They cannot profitably occupy their
machinery and capital in refining sugar for " savages in

Owhyee" and other outlandish places. They will find themselves obliged to join the agreement of the Convention.

Sir Thomas Farrer troubles himself, and wants to trouble us, about the fluctuations of the markets of the future. We have confidence in restoring the trade to its natural channels, and in giving everybody interested a fair field and no favour.

Sir Thomas Farrer wishes to know how it will be possible ever again to impose a duty upon sugar. This would be setting back the hands of the clock as much as if it were proposed to re-enact the sliding-scale system for wheat. In fact, such arguments are like making "cages for gnats, and chains to yoke a flea."

We working-men are very thankful for what the Government, despising jealousy and misrepresentation, are doing on our behalf in this most intricate and difficult negotiation. We beg the Government to persevere—to "go in and win," as Sheridan said to his soldiers at the fall of Richmond. We could not refer to better advice than the words of the Preacher—" He that observeth the wind shall not sow ; and he that regardeth the clouds shall not reap."

Yours respectfully,

GEORGE SHUTE,

Member of the Executive of the London Workmen's Anti-Sugar Bounty Association.

Thames Sugar Refinery, Silvertown, E., October 27

APPENDIX D.

LETTER TO LORD SALISBURY FROM LEADING REPRE-
SENTATIVES OF ALL BRANCHES OF THE HOME,
COLONIAL, AND FOREIGN SUGAR TRADE, ON THE
PRICE OF SUGAR.

Billiter House, London, E.C.,
11th December, 1888.

The Most Honourable THE MARQUIS OF SALISBURY,
K.G., &c. &c.

My Lord Marquis,

I have the honour to convey to your Lordship the
enclosed letter, embodying an expression of opinion by
those entitled to speak with great authority upon the
subject, as to the effect the abolition of bounties, provided
for in the Convention, will have upon the supply of sugar
in the United Kingdom, and the price to be paid by the
consumer.

In commending this letter to your Lordship's kind
attention I am to point out its thoroughly representative
character, the signatures comprising those who are engaged
in the sugar-refining industry in the United Kingdom, as
well as those interested in the growth and production of
sugar in the British Colonies, and other countries, including
the East Indies and Java, the West Indies and British
Guiana, Mauritius, Natal, Queensland, New South Wales,
Fiji, Cuba, and Brazil. The representatives of the
engineering and other industries in the United Kingdom
have also expressed their concurrence.

It may be asked, if we as producers, merchants, and
traders do not believe that present prices will be raised by

the abolition of bounties, why should we be so active in promoting that abolition? To such an enquiry we reply, that our interest lies not in raising prices but in depriving our competitors of the cash bounty, as an addition to the amount of the market price—whatever that may be—which enables them to obtain a higher real price than our producers, and therefore to increase and improve their production to our detriment, while we are conversely, from the same cause, precluded from increasing and improving to the same extent. In short, our interest requires that all producers should recoup their cost of production solely and only from the market price of the whole world's competition, so that all producers may have the same opportunity and the same inducement to progress in proportion with the increase of consumption.

At present, whatever the price may be, we are still hindered by the prospect of bounty-fed competition from making the progress which under natural conditions we undoubtedly should make. So long as the price of sugar depends upon such uncertain and fluctuating conditions as are brought about by the bounty system, prudent capitalists are necessarily reluctant to invest capital in the industry.

I have, &c.,

(Signed) N. LUBBOCK,

Chairman of the West India Committee and of the British and Colonial Anti-Bounty Association.

30th November, 1888.

The Most Honourable THE MARQUIS OF SALISBURY, K.G., &c.

My Lord Marquis,

We venture respectfully to address your Lordship upon the main objection which has been raised to the

Sugar Bounties Convention, viz.: that its effect will be to raise the price of sugar to the consumer.

We claim to speak with authority upon this subject, inasmuch as we represent the Home Industry connected with sugar refining, the sugar-producing industry of the British Colonies and other countries, also the engineering and other industries in the United Kingdom connected with the production, manufacture, and distribution of sugar. Indeed, we practically represent the whole of the British Sugar Industry, in all its various departments both at home and abroad.

We are, therefore, thoroughly acquainted practically with the cost of producing and refining sugar, and we can unhesitatingly express our conviction, that the coming into force of the proposed Convention, and the consequent abolition of bounties, will not raise the price of sugar above its present level, nor will there be any restriction in the quantity of sugar imported into this country.

We have, &c.

The following is the list of names attached to the above letter :—

N. Lubbock, Chairman of the West India Committee and the British and Colonial Anti-Bounty Association.

James Duncan, Chairman of the British Sugar Refiners' Committee.

Hogg, Curtis, Campbell & Co., Proprietors and Merchants, West Indies and British Guiana.

Robert Kerr, Chairman, Scottish Sugar Refiners' Association.

Tom Neill, Honorary Secretary, Scottish Refiners' Association.

Abram Lyle & Sons, Sugar Refiners, London.

George Martineau, Honorary Secretary, British Sugar Refiners' Committee.

Thomas Daniel & Co., Limited, Edward Chambers, Director, Proprietors and Merchants, West Indies and British Guiana.

The Rt. Hon. E. P. Bouverie, Chairman of the Colonial Company, Limited.

Maclaine, Watson & Co., Merchants, London and Java.

Smith, Wood & Co., Merchants, London and Manila.

Arbuthnot, Latham & Co., Merchants, London.

C. Czarnikow, Sugar Broker, London.

Thomas J. Johnston, Director of the St. Lucia Central Sugar Factory Company, Limited.

Jas. Child, Chairman of the Aerated Bread Company, London.

Sir Thomas Thornhill, Bart., Barbados.

C. Tennant, Sons & Co., London and Trinidad.

Thomson, Hankey & Co., Merchants, London.

Daniel de Pass, Sugar Planter, Natal, South Africa.

C. Washington Eves, Sugar Planter, Jamaica.

E. D. & F. Man, Sugar and Colonial Brokers.

Cottam & Hill, Sugar and Colonial Brokers.

C. & C. J. Coles, Sugar and Colonial Brokers.

J. V. Drake & Co., 10 and 11, Mincing Lane, and Magdeburg Sugar Merchants.

The Dennery Co., Limited: the St. Lucia Usines and Estates Co.; A. H. Hales, Manager, Sugar Producers, S. Lucia, W.I.

J. & E. Williams, Sugar Merchants and Brokers, Mincing Lane, London; and Magdeburg.

Carey and Browne, Produce Brokers, 36, Mincing Lane.

William Anderson & Co., 10, Mincing Lane, Sugar and Colonial Brokers.

Macdonald, Hutcheson & Co., London and Greenock, Sugar Brokers.

C. M. & C. Woodhouse, Sugar Brokers.

Livens & Bishop, 27, Mincing Lane, Sugar Brokers.

L. Cowan & Sons, Hammersmith Bridge Works, and 7, Mincing Lane, Sugar Refiners.

Ed. Kynaston, 10, Mincing Lane, Sugar Broker.

Bieber & Co., 4, Fenchurch Avenue, London and Brazil, Merchants.

Mee, Billing & Co, 9, Great St. Helen's, London and Brazil, Merchants.

Raggio-Carneiro & Co., 129A, Winchester House, London and Brazil, Merchants.

James Keiller & Sons, Manufacturing Confectioners, Marmalade and Preserve Makers, Dundee and London.

Erdmann & Sielcker, Merchants, London and Java.

Blyth, Greene, Jourdain & Co., London and Mauritius.

Sendall and Wade, Merchants and Proprietors, St. Kitts, W.I.

J. C. Shaw, Madras, East Indies.

Sir Daniel Cooper, Bart., G.C.M.G., for Australia, New Zealand, and Fiji.

Young, Ehlers & Co., Merchants and Proprietors, London and Australia.

Boddington & Co., Merchants and Proprietors, West Indies and British Guiana.

D. Larnach, Banker and Proprietor, Australia.

Jno. McConnell & Co., British Guiana, Proprietors and Merchants, London and Liverpool.

For the Natal Central Sugar Company, Limited. D. Dors, Managing Director.

R. J. Jeffray, for Queensland and Victoria.

James B. Alliott, for Messrs. Manlove, Alliott & Co., Limited, Engineers and Manufacturers.

Hermann Voss for the Anglo-Continental (late Ohlendorff's) Guano Works, Limited.

Charles Parbury, Proprietor and Merchant, Australia.

F. Parbury & Co., Proprietors and Merchants, London and Australia.

p.p. George Fletcher & Co., W. Parratt, Engineers and Manufacturers, London and Derby.

Sandbach, Tinne & Co., West India Planters and Merchants, Liverpool.

Alex. Garnett & Co., West India Planters and Merchants, Liverpool.

Sir T. Edwards Moss, Bart., West India Planter, Otterspool.

Bushby, Son & Beazley, Sugar Brokers, Liverpool.

Edward H. Harrison & Son, Produce Brokers, Liverpool.

Nichs. Waterhouse & Sons,   do.

Fairrie, Astley & Co.,   do.

Brancker, Boxwell & Co.,   do.

Hampshire, Turner & Co.,   do.

A. Litherland Jones & Co.,   do.

Macfie & Sons, Sugar Refiners, Liverpool.

Henry Tate & Sons,   do.

For Fairrie & Co., Limited, James Fairrie, Sugar Refiners, Liverpool.

James Leitch & Co., Sugar Refiners, Liverpool.

Jos. Heap & Sons,   do.

For the Sankey Sugar Company, Edward C. Turner (partner), Sugar Refiners, Liverpool.

G. Jager & Sons, Sugar Refiners, Liverpool.

Crosfield, Barrow & Co.,   do.

George Crosfield & Co., Sugar Merchants, Liverpool.

Anthony Jones & Co.,   do.

Edward P. Parry & Co.,   do.

APPENDIX E.

THE MOST-FAVOURED - NATION CLAUSE, BY W. P. B. SHEPHEARD, ESQ., OF LINCOLN'S INN, BARRISTER-AT-LAW. (1879.)

THE whole question of the character and consequences of the sugar bounties was thoroughly investigated by a Select Committee of the House of Commons in 1879, and a report was issued by that Committee on the 4th of August, 1880.

Shortly after the labours of the Parliamentary Committee were concluded, a further attempt to bring about an international settlement was made by Her Majesty's Government. But the French Government, early in 1881, met the proposals of Her Majesty's Government for an international conference to put an end to bounties by insisting on a preliminary understanding as to the admissibility of the principle of levying countervailing duties against sugars which might be exported under bounty by other States not adopting the conclusions of the conference.

This preliminary basis — which the experience of previous conferences had shown to be essential for an international agreement — was at once rejected by Her Majesty's then Government, and thereupon the matter dropped.

During subsequent negotiations for the renewal of a commercial treaty with France the necessity of some express stipulations as to export bounties was urged upon the British Commissioners by persons interested in the sugar trade. But with the failure of those negotiations the opportunity of raising the question passed away.

It remains therefore to be considered whether the provisions of existing treaties are not materially affected by any State granting export bounties.

By commercial treaties [see List of Treaties of Commerce and Navigation. Commercial No. 27, 1879 (c. 2424)] various States have granted to, and secured from, Great Britain the treatment of the most favoured nation. Under the most-favoured-nation articles in these treaties each treaty State is entitled to receive the same treatment as that accorded to the nation most favoured by the other treaty State.

Such article does not in terms preclude a State from favouring its own subjects; but this liberty, it is submitted, must be limited by some principles of international relations, and any exercise of such liberty in a way to endanger the interests of other States would be just ground for diplomatic remonstrance. This liberty of advancing the interests of its own subjects is independent of all treaties—is, in fact, inherent in the independence of one Sovereign Power to exercise natural rights without reference to other Sovereign Powers. To what extent, then, is this liberty cut down by such an engagement as that which arises when two Powers mutually accord one to the other most-favoured-nation treatment? For the purpose of illustration, let it be assumed that Great Britain and France are bound by the engagement of a treaty to give the one to the other most-favoured-nation treatment. It is clear, then, that neither State so bound can give any other State exclusive favours. To this extent, then, the inherent liberty of each State is restricted by the treaty engagement. It is necessary clearly to understand that the *rights* and *duties* of each contracting State in respect of this engagement are, as regards *rights*, to be enjoyed *within the territory of the other State*, and as regards *duties* to be *performed* within *its own territory*. France, for instance, is to enjoy the right of favoured-nation treatment within British territory, and to perform the duty of according that treatment to Great Britain within French territory. The right is satisfied in accordance with the treaty when France receives within British territory the same treatment as the nation most favoured by Great Britain. If, for instance, Great Britain were to give a bounty on all goods *imported* from Germany the rights of France would be at once interfered with. But if Germany gave an *export* bounty the economic consequence to France would be identical with that which would follow from Great Britain giving an *import* bounty on goods from Germany. In either case German exporters would possess a State favour which was wanting to French exporters, and such State favour would be operative upon the competition between France and Germany on the markets of Great Britain. An identical result would follow if Great Britain levied a greater import duty against goods from France than on those from Germany when the conditions of export were the same in both countries. In the foregoing illustration of *three* methods of producing the *consequences of differential treatment*, two are clearly forbidden by the terms of the most-favoured-nation article—viz.: 1. The grant by Great Britain of an exclusive import bounty on goods from Germany. 2. The imposition by Great Britain of a higher duty on goods imported from France than on those from Germany, conditions of export being the same in both countries.

But in the third case—viz., of Germany granting an *export* bounty on her own goods, the consequences to France are the same as those which would have resulted from Great Britain having violated the terms of the most-favoured-nation article by either of the two methods just referred to. One result from the action of Germany in giving export bounties would be to diminish the trade between Great Britain and France intended to be facilitated by their reciprocal engagements under the most-favoured-nation article.

The favoured-nation article as a treaty compact enables Great Britain to obtain the benefit of the conventional as distinguished from the general tariff of many foreign States, and in return those States,—this country having one uniform tariff,—can only rely upon Great Britain maintaining a firm opposition to all attempts on the part of any foreign State to vary in its own favour the equality of the international competing basis intended to be secured by the terms of the most-favoured-nation article. It is clear, therefore, that an export bounty by any one State is a direct diminution of the value of the reciprocal considerations which enable Great Britain to secure the benefits of most-favoured-nation treatment from various other States. Upon these grounds Great Britain, it is submitted, might protest to Germany, with whom a like engagement has been entered into, that the grant of such export bounties was productive of consequences which were identical with the consequences which would ensue to French and other foreign commerce if Great Britain herself violated her favoured-nation engagements with foreign Powers, and thus operated to render those engagements of Great Britain more or less valueless.

If, in the foregoing illustration, there be substituted for France all the States possessing most-favoured-nation engagements with Great Britain the argument is applicable. Many States, instead of one State, suffer consequences economically analogous to the evils of the differential

L

treatment which the terms of the most-favoured-nation article purport to prevent.

The sum and substance of the argument come to this. Whilst on the one hand the favoured-nation article does not restrict the liberty of either contracting Power to favour its national productions, yet, on the other hand, if it favours them by export bounties consequences result to the various most-favoured-nation engagements of the other contracting Power which deprive them of their value as effectually as if specifically violated. The argument can, however, be carried no higher. It is absolutely conclusive as to the economic analogy between the effects on international competition of an export bounty and a differential duty; it is fairly conclusive that the favoured-nation article gives either of two contracting Powers the right to complain of an export bounty by the other contracting Power, on the grounds that such form of protection affects the value of similar engagements with other Powers. Passing from argument to authority, we would first refer to the responsible position taken up by the Government of the United States in dealing with a difficulty arising out of the interpretation of this very clause, as far back as 1822, in connection with the treaty of 1803, for the cession by France of Louisiana to the United States.

Art. VIII. of that treaty was as follows: "À l'avenir et pour toujours après l'expiration des douze années susdites les navires Français seront traités sur le pied de la nation la plus favorisée dans les ports ci-dessus mentionnés."

All conditions are absent from this article. Nevertheless, conditions were claimed as of right by the United States. What the conditions were has no bearing on the *principle of interpretation*, upon which point alone we refer to this international dispute.

The cause of the dispute was the advantage enjoyed by Great Britain in respect of her vessels being placed upon the same footing as the vessels of the United States, whilst vessels from France were subjected to heavy tonnage duties upon entering the American ports, including those of Louisiana. The question is thus referred to in the official report of Committee of Commerce, communicated to the House of Representatives, 15th March, 1822 :—

" France. The extra duties imposed in 1817 by the French Government on the produce of the United States, when imported into France in vessels of the United States, have excluded them from a competition with French vessels carrying American produce to France. Feeling the injustice of such impositions on the part of France, the merchants memorialised Congress. On consideration of their complaints, an Act passed the 15th May, 1820, subjecting French vessels entering the ports of the United States to a tonnage duty of eighteen dollars a ton after the 1st July, 1820."

The facts which appear to have originated the contest may be concisely summarised thus :— The United States were under obligation to treat the ships of France upon the footing of the most favoured nation in the ports of Louisiana. It is important to notice that this treaty obligation has no conditions specified. But it would appear that at that date (1820) British vessels entering the ports, say of New Orleans, were admitted on the same terms as American vessels, whilst those of France were subjected to a heavy tonnage duty. Surely upon the words of the Treaty the French could plead their right to the same treatment as British vessels in the ports of the ceded territory. It was part of the consideration for the cession. And yet the claim was disallowed by the President of the United States, and why ? We will let the President state

his own case as it appears in his Fifth Annual Message of
3rd December, 1821.

"It is my duty to state, as a cause of very great regret,
that very serious differences have occurred in this negotiation, respecting the construction of the Eighth Article
of the Treaty of 1803, by which Louisiana was ceded to
the United States, and likewise, respecting the seizure of
the *Apollo* in 1820, for a violation of our revenue laws.
The claim of the Government of France has excited
not less surprise than concern, because there does
not appear to be a just foundation for it in either
instance. By the Eighth Article of the Treaty referred to
it is stipulated that, after the expiration of twelve years
during which time it was provided by the Seventh or preceding Article that the vessels of France and Spain should
be admitted into the ports of the ceded territory, without
paying higher duties on merchandise, or tonnage on the
vessels, than such as were paid by citizens of the United
States, the ships of France should for ever afterwards be
placed on the footing of the most favoured nation. By the
obvious construction of this Article, it is presumed that it
was intended that no favour should be granted to any
Power, in those ports, to which France should not be forth-
with entitled; nor should any accommodation be allowed
to another Power, on conditions to which she would not
also be entitled on the same conditions. Under this
construction no favour or accommodation could be
granted to any Power to the prejudice of France.
By allowing the equivalent allowed by those Powers,
she would always stand in those ports on the footing of
the most favoured nation. But if this Article should be so
construed as that France should enjoy of right, and without paying the equivalent, all the advantages of such conditions as might be allowed to other Powers in return for

important concessions made by them, then the whole
character of the stipulation would be changed. She would
not only be placed on the footing of the most favoured
nation, but on a footing held by no other nation. She
would enjoy all advantages allowed to them, in consideration of like advantages allowed to us, free from any and
every condition whatsoever."

By the following quotation from the President's Sixth
Annual Message of 3rd December, 1822, the dispute
appears to have terminated in France concluding a treaty
of commerce :—

"On the 24th June last a Convention of Navigation
and Commerce was concluded in this city between the
United States and France, by ministers duly authorised for
the purpose. The sanction of the Executive having been
given to this Convention under a conviction that, taking all
its stipulations into view, it rested essentially on a basis of
reciprocal and equal advantage, I deemed it my duty, in
compliance with the authority vested in the Executive by
the second section of the Act of the last session of the
6th May, concerning navigation, to suspend by proclama-
tion, until the end of the next session of Congress, the
operation of the Act entitled, 'An Act to impose a new
tonnage duty on French ships and vessels, and for other
purposes,' and to suspend likewise all other duties on
French vessels, or the goods imported in them, which ex-
ceeded the duties on American vessels, and on similar
goods imported in them."

Now in Wheaton's "Elements of International Law" this
dispute is referred to in connection with the principle laid
down by this Jurist on the " Interpretation of Treaties."
The reference appears as a foot-note to the following
passage in the text. " Public treaties are to be interpreted
like other laws and contracts. Such is the inevitable

imperfection and ambiguity of all human language that the mere words alone of any writing, literally expounded, will go a very little way towards explaining its meaning. Certain technical rules of interpretation have, therefore, been adopted by writers on ethics and public law to explain the meaning of international compacts in cases of doubt."

The note in Wheaton, by the Editor, Mr. Lawrence, does not give the views taken by the President which we have quoted, but contains the following passage from Mr. Adams' note to the French Minister, meeting his demand that orders might be issued to such effect that in future the 8th article of the Treaty of Cession should receive its entire execution, and that the advantages granted to Great Britain in all the ports of the United States might be secured to France in those of Louisiana. To that demand Mr. Adams replied that he was instructed to say " that the vessels of France are treated in the ports of Louisiana upon the footing of ' *the most favoured nation*,' and that neither the English nor any other foreign nation enjoys gratuitous advantage which is not equally enjoyed by France. But English vessels, by virtue of a conditional compact, are admitted into the ports of the United States, including those of Louisiana, upon payments of the same duties as the vessels of the United States."

The sum and substance then of this historic episode, which we have detailed from official documents, amount to this : viz., that notwithstanding the absence of all conditions from the words of the Louisiana Treaty, yet conditions were imported into its interpretation by the United States.

In 1878 a debate in the House of Commons upon the favoured-nation clause contains some valuable authority upon its proper interpretation.

To make the debate intelligible, as bearing upon the

point we are now discussing, we must explain that the
Contagious Diseases (Animals) Bill, as introduced by the
Government, subjected cattle from foreign countries to
compulsory slaughter, with power to the Privy Council to
release the Channel Islands and the Isle of Man from
restriction ; and, as regards Canada and America, excepted
these countries from restriction until an order was made
by the Privy Council with respect to these excepted
countries.

American cattle would, therefore have been free until
subjected to provisions for compulsory slaughter by order
in Council. Consequently, as between foreign countries
generally and America, inequality of condition would have
been specifically created had the Bill become Law. The
inequality would have arisen from the fact that America
would have been free until the Privy Council issued an
order ; whilst as regards other foreign countries, immunity
from disease would not have freed them from restriction
until an Act of Parliament was passed. The Government
introduced an amendment, enabling the Privy Council to
exempt Denmark, Sweden, Norway, Spain, or Portugal.
Still, inequality of conditions would have remained. This
inequality raised a debate on the " favoured-nation clause."
In the course of the debate, which we only propose to
follow so far as it contains direct opinion on the favoured-
nation clause, Sir Henry James, who raised the question,
pointed out the inequality in the provisions we have referred
to, and consequent violation of the " favoured-nation clause."

Sir Charles W. Dilke observed " that it would not
be in the power of the Privy Council, under this Bill,
to admit French cattle, even although France was entirely free from disease, while it would be in the power
of the Privy Council to admit the cattle of countries that
competed with France ; and, therefore, with like freedom

from disease, there could not be a like principle of treatment applicable to all cases." Upon this inequality Sir Charles W. Dilke rested his arguments against the Bill as violating the favoured-nation clauses.

The Attorney-General (Sir John Holker) said, "Now, what was the meaning of the 'favoured-nation clause?' He took it that in whatever language that clause might be expressed—and the language of the different treaties was not always the same—but, whatever language might be used, the real meaning was this, 'You, Great Britain, shall treat us in the same way as you treat the most favoured nation with whom you have a treaty, that is to say, you shall treat us as well as you treat them under the like circumstances.' . . . Really and truly, then, the favoured-nation clause meant that which was expressed in the case of Austria, namely, that neither of the high contracting Powers or parties should establish a prohibition of importation, exportation, or transit against the other which should not, 'under like circumstances' be applicable to the third country most favoured in this respect."

Sir William Harcourt said the Attorney-General's "whole argument was founded on the very points for which those who opposed the Bill had contended . . . The Attorney-General had laid down the principle that in the most-favoured-nation clause they must, under similar circumstances, deal with all countries alike. He (Sir William Harcourt) was not going to quarrel with that proposition, though, if strictly interpreted, it would be found not to be quite correct."

Referring to the bounty on loaf sugar, Sir William Harcourt said :—" They were bound to admit this sugar, under similar circumstances, from different countries ; but they had great difficulty with France when a bonus was given by France itself upon this sugar. They might have

said the circumstances were not similar in a country which
gave a bonus on their sugar, and therefore they would not
admit it.   But it would not be politic to maintain a proposition to that extent . . . What a nation could claim
under the 'favoured-nation clause' was that there should be
an immediate power under similar circumstances to admit
it to equal rights with others."

The present Lord Chancellor, then the Solicitor-
General, observed "that the 'favoured-nation clause'
assured equality of rights to all the parties concerned,
but the mistake was to say that that involved identity
of treatment."

Lord, then Mr., Herschell "quite agreed with the hon.
and learned Solicitor-General that equality of right did
not necessarily mean identity of treatment.   But he did
say that equality of right did mean identity of treatment
under similar circumstances.",

Sir John, then Mr., Gorst said : " Now, what we had
promised to do [under our treaties] was, not to establish
any prohibition of importation or transit against the
produce of any country with which we had entered into
treaties containing the 'most-favoured-nation clause'
which would not under like circumstances be applicable
to all other countries."

The Chancellor of the Exchequer said "That this
country was bound to treat all foreign nations alike—
but that was, alike under similar circumstances."

Mr. Gladstone observed that " he would say one word
upon the doctrine of similar circumstances.   He did not
deny that it was a doctrine that could not utterly be excluded from discussion of that kind. . . . ' Similar circumstances' were very large words ; they admitted of infinite
discretion in interpretation." Referring to a most-favoured-
nation treaty, Mr. Gladstone said :—" Did not the treaty

mean that there should be immediate equality ? What he
concluded was that it did mean that there should be immediate equality."

It is not necessary to add to this valuable body of
opinion. Sir William Harcourt and Mr. Gladstone properly qualified the doctrine of "like circumstances" from
too great an extension.

The upshot of the debate was the withdrawal by the
Government of all distinction between foreign countries,
by subjecting all alike to provisions of compulsory slaughter,
with power to the Privy Council to exempt any countries
upon being satisfied as to freedom from disease.

The principle of the Contagious Diseases (Animals)
Act of 1878 was to exclude, not cattle, but disease. To
exclude protection from our markets is all that our sugar
industry need contend for. It is impossible to suppose we
are precluded from excluding protection by any favoured-
nation clause, otherwise this clause in the last Austrian
treaty would render nugatory all the efforts of our Government for the abolition of bounties.

It is on the markets that the provisions of commercial
treaties are meant to have, and must have, their effect.
Our national policy is to secure free trade competition.
As regards foreign markets, we admit our inability to
do more than obtain, when we can, the "most-favoured-
nation treatment." Against protection for the national
industries of foreigners on their home markets we are
powerless. But we venture to say that the true spirit
of our commercial treaties will be violated if, on our own
home market, our national production may be harassed by
foreign States claiming, under those treaties, unrestricted
right of entry for their products when heavily subsidised
by export bounties. Such a claim has never yet been
advanced by any foreign State in the discussion of this

question. Moreover, such foreign States as give bounties harass not only our own home and colonial production, but the production of other foreign States in treaty with us, who give no bounties. Indeed, in Mr. C. M. Kennedy's letter to Lord Derby of the 21st April, 1874, we find that M. Descilligny, the French Minister of Commerce, had stated "that bounties avowed or disguised, granted by foreign Powers, might be checked by a general provision of English law to impose a duty on sugar imported from foreign countries which are held to give bounties on exportation."

In 1879 this question was referred by persons interested to the late Professor Sheldon Amos, of the Inner Temple, and Mr. Shepheard, of Lincoln's Inn, and their opinion was as follows :—

"The question submitted to us is whether the imposition by Great Britain of a countervailing duty against sugar upon the export of which a bounty was obtained, whilst sugar upon which no bounty was obtained was subjected to no such duty, would contravene the most-favoured-nation clauses of existing commercial treaties.

" Before considering the question from a juridical point of view, it is necessary to settle the meaning of the term 'bounty.' For the purpose of this opinion we confine the term bounty to that proportion of drawback which is in excess of actual duty paid. It is not necessary to discuss how such excess arises, but it is evident that when a State returns on all exported sugar a particular amount by way of 'drawback,' and such amount is in excess of the duty actually levied, such excess amount constitutes an actual premium or bounty on exportation.

" An exporter from a foreign country receiving such a bounty becomes an importer into this country, possessing a tariff or fiscal advantage over other importers not enjoying a bounty. This seems such an obvious economic consequence that we are entitled to assume it as such without discussing purely economic points.

"Although this tariff advantage is not created by the importing State, yet it can only be enjoyed by the foreign exporter upon sufferance of the importing State, therefore such tariff advantage virtually depends upon the negative action of the importing State.

"We also assume that the countervailing duty to which our opinion is to apply is a duty which shall correspond in amount to the bounty as defined. We further assume that if such a bounty as defined be met by such a duty as defined, the importer enjoying such bounty, but liable in consequence to such duty, is thereby in no different fiscal position to an importer enjoying no bounty and paying no duty.

"These points are such as must be established by economic reasoning, and for the purpose of this opinion we are asked to assume them, and we do so without expressing our opinion as to their validity on economic grounds.

"For the purpose of illustrating the arguments which lead to our conclusion we propose to take the Treaty of Commerce between Her Britannic Majesty and His Majesty the Emperor of Austria of 1876. This treaty was for one year, and expired on the 31st of December, 1877, but previous to such expiration was renewed by a subsequent treaty of 26th November, 1877, from year to year, at a year's notice of denunciation from either side from any date. We understand that the treaty so renewed is still in force.

"The 1st Article of the Treaty defines the rights of the subjects of either sovereign power resident in the territories of the other.

"The 2nd Article is as follows:

ARTICLE II.

" The produce and manufactures of, as well as all goods coming from Austria-Hungary, which are imported into the territories and possessions, including the colonies and foreign possessions, of Her Britannic Majesty, and the produce and manufactures of, as well as all goods coming from, British possessions, which are imported into the Austro-Hungarian monarchy, whether intended for consumption, warehousing, re-exportation, or transit, shall therein, during the continuance of this treaty, be treated in the same manner as, and in particular shall be subjected to no higher or other duties than, the produce and goods of any third country the most favoured in this respect.

" No other or higher duties shall be levied in the Austro-Hungarian monarchy on the exportation of any goods to the territories and possessions, including the colonies and foreign possessions, of Her Britannic Majesty, or in the territories and possessions, including the colonies and foreign possessions, of Her Britannic Majesty, on the exportation of any goods to the Austro-Hungarian monarchy, than on the exportation of the like goods to any third country the most favoured in this respect.

" The two high contracting parties likewise guarantee to each other treatment on the footing of the most favoured third country, in regard to the transit of goods through the territory of the one from and to the territory of the other.

" The 3rd Article is as follows :—

ARTICLE III.

" Every reduction in the tariff of import and export duties, as well as every favour or immunity that one of the contracting parties grants to the subjects and commerce of a third Power, shall be participated in simultaneously and unconditionally by the other.

" The 4th Article is as follows :—

ARTICLE IV.

" The stipulations of the foregoing Articles, I. to III., relative to the reciprocal treatment on the footing of the most favoured third country, shall not apply—

" 1. To those special and ancient privileges which are accorded to Turkish subjects for the Turkish trade in Austria-Hungary.

" 2. To those advantages which are or may be granted on the part of the Austro-Hungarian monarchy to the neighbouring countries solely for the purpose of facilitating the frontier traffic, or to those reductions of, or exemptions from, customs duties which are only valid in the said monarchy for certain frontiers, or for the inhabitants of certain districts.

" 3. To the obligations imposed upon either of the high contracting parties by a Customs Union already concluded, or which may hereafter be concluded.

" The 5th Article is as follows :—

ARTICLE V.

" Neither of the high contracting parties shall establish a prohibition of importation, exportation, or transit against the other which shall not, under like circumstances, be applicable to the third country most favoured in this respect.

" The 6th Article refers to trade-marks, &c.

" The 7th Article determines the duration of treaty.

" And the 8th Article provides as to its ratification.

" From the foregoing it appears that our opinion must be

governed by the interpretation to be placed on Article II., which may be concisely described as a favoured-nation importing and exporting clause.

"We are of opinion that, under this clause, Her Majesty has become bound (*inter alia*) to accord to Austria every advantage in respect of her exports to this country accorded to the most favoured third country; and this equality of fiscal conditions between such most favoured third country and Austria, the latter State must be taken to have accepted as the basis of the compact.

"Moreover, Her Majesty has been likewise bound to same effect by similar clauses in other treaties to France, Germany, Belgium, Italy, &c. The result, then, of these respective obligations can only be attained by the produce of each of the several exporting countries being admitted on terms of fiscal equality into this country. If, therefore, one of such exporting countries destroys this equality by giving a fiscal advantage which it is within the power of this country to neutralise, we consider that the interpretation of this clause would favour rather than preclude the exercise of such power.

"Independently of all treaties, each country has full power to deal with importations from other countries on any terms it pleases—to exclude some and to favour others. The favoured-nation clause is a restriction upon this power, in order to bring about equality of fiscal conditions between the importers from either treaty Power and importers from third countries into the territories of the other treaty Power.

"Moreover, it is clear that the articles of a treaty of commerce are directed to the interests of classes of the subjects of the respective Sovereign Powers in their several characters as importers, exporters, &c. Therefore the injurious operation of any State tariff or fiscal arrangements upon importers, exporters, &c., in their respective characters as such, raises a proper question under the treaty. And in our opinion, it is not the less a treaty question, because it may happen that the fiscal action which prejudices some one class of citizens in their treaty characters may benefit some other class. Therefore, we are of opinion that imports of sugar into this country may, without contravening the favoured-nation clauses of existing commercial treaties, be distinguished as to countries of origin wherein bounties on export are or are not obtainable, and a countervailing duty levied on sugar imported from countries where export bounties are obtainable, whilst sugar from all other countries is admitted duty free. This construction is consistent with the fact that the Sugar Convention of 1864 between Great Britain, France, Holland, and Belgium contained an article admitting the principle of the imposition of a differential surtax against countries not parties to that Convention, giving export bounties, notwithstanding that at the date of that Convention this country was bound by treaty with Russia to admit her products at no "other or higher duties than are or shall be payable on the like article the growth, produce, or manufacture of any other foreign country." [See Treaty of Commerce with Russia, 1859, Art. 2.]

"Moreover, notwithstanding such article in the Convention of 1864, favoured-nation clauses were contained in the commercial treaties entered into during the period of ten years for which that Convention was in force ; and such favoured-nation clauses must be held as subject to the treaty engagements under which, during such period, Great Britain was subject by that Convention of 1864.

"In conclusion, we beg to state that our opinion is based upon the broad principle that equality of fiscal condition, as between either Treaty Power and any third country the

most favoured by the other Treaty Power, is the object of
favoured-nation clauses, and that the one who destroys such
equality cannot appeal to the treaty against the act necessitated to reinstate that equality.

"(*Signed*)   SHELDON AMOS, of the Inner Temple
                 Barrister-at-Law.

" Professor of Jurisprudence to the Council of Legal Education of
    Inns of Court for three years ending 1875, and late Professor
    of Jurisprudence to University Coll., London.

"(*Signed*)   WALLWYN POVER B. SHEPHEARD, of
                 Linc. Inn, Barrister-at-Law.

" July 22nd, 187 ."

APPENDIX F.

THE SUGAR CONVENTION.

To the Editor of "The Times."

SIR,—Lord Bramwell desires to prove that the price of sugar must rise if bounties are abolished ; and his proof would be perfectly correct if the sugar market had arrived at the point he imagines, namely, below the level, to use his own words, of "the average rate of profit." But he overlooks the fact that, if we had arrived at that point, those producers who receive no bounty, and who at present are supplying the world with 2,400,000 tons a year, would have "discontinued production," having already got below that level. It is to avoid that calamity, which would be a great injury to the community at large as well as to the producers in particular, that we urge the abolition of bounties. Lord Bramwell's argument is clearly based on the assumption that the market has already been driven down by bounties to the level of the cost of production. He says : "This is obviously a bounty on exportation. The result is that the sugar is cheaper here than in the country where it is made, not only by the tax which consumers there pay, *but by the extra sum paid in drawbacks."* He assumes that the drawback is given away to the buyer; in other words, that cost price has been reached. If there were any doubt on this point, it would be set at rest by what follows at the end of the argument, where Lord Bramwell says :—

"At present the German producer can sell his sugar at a certain price because he gets the bounty. He gets no more than the average rate of profit on this capital, or competition would bring his price down. Then when the bounty is taken away, to get that average profit he must raise his price. He will do so, or discontinue his production."

If the world were supplied entirely with bounty-fed sugar, this would be an exact description of the situation, and we should be most foolish to desire the abolition of the bounty. But, as it is, the world is supplied with 2,800,000 tons of bounty-fed sugar and 2,400,000 tons of sugar which receives no bounty. If we had arrived at the price imagined by Lord Bramwell, the producer who received no bounty would, as Lord Bramwell says of the bounty-fed producer when he loses his bounty, "discontinue his production," since he would be unable, owing to the bounty-fed competition, to fall back on the alternative of raising his price.

This position will be reached if bounties continue ; we were close upon it in 1884, the period so well described by Sir Thomas Farrer as one of "glut, collapse, and ruin." It is to avert the stoppage of the natural sources of production that we advocate the abolition of bounties, and we do so on the broad grounds of the interest of the consumer no less than on the narrower grounds of the interest of the producer.

At present the market price of sugar is far removed from the level imagined by Lord Bramwell, and therefore his reasoning does not apply. If production were flowing in its natural channels unhindered by the incubus of an artificial competition, sugar would be cheaper instead of dearer than it is now. At the present moment the whole world is suffering, in the increased cost of sugar, for having

become too dependent on one particular source of supply
—a dependence artificially brought about by the bounty
system.

The following is a quotation from a market report of
last Saturday, in proof of this assertion :—" It is now
evidently, as was foreseen might be the case, that the
holders on the Continent have the immediate future of the
market much in their hands, owing to the reduction of
stocks in Europe and America, as well as the decrease in
some of the leading sources of cane production."   In other
words, the beetroot producers can corner the market.

GEORGE MARTINEAU.

21, Mincing Lane, E.C.,
   April 3rd, 1889.

PRINTED BY CASSELL & COMPANY, LIMITED, LA BELLE SAUVAGE, LONDON, E.C.